pushing at the boundaries of unity

Anglicans and Baptists in conversation

Faith and Unity Executive Committee
of the Baptist Union of Great Britain

The Council for Christian Unity
of the Church of England

CHURCH HOUSE
PUBLISHING

Church House Publishing
Church House
Great Smith Street
London SW1P 3NZ

Tel: 020 7898 1451
Fax: 020 7898 1449

ISBN 0 7151 4052 3

GS Misc 801

A report of the informal
conversations between the Council
for Christian Unity of the Church of
England and the Faith and Unity
Executive of the Baptist Union of
Great Britain

This report has only the authority of
the commission that prepared it.

Published 2005 for the Council for
Christian Unity of the Archbishops'
Council and the Baptist Union of
Great Britain by Church House
Publishing

Typeset in Franklin Gothic 9.5/11pt

Printed in England by
The Cromwell Press Ltd,
Trowbridge, Wiltshire

contents

introduction

Representatives of the Baptist Union of Great Britain, appointed by its Faith and Unity Executive Committee, and representatives of the Church of England, appointed by its Council for Christian Unity, met on 20 occasions between May 1992 and January 2005. The attached report to our parent bodies gives some account of these discussions.

The informal conversations were interesting and informative. We were all encouraged by the degree of agreement that exists between us and by the fact that there are many places in England and throughout the world where Anglicans and Baptists are working closely together. We valued the friendship and trust between members of the group which allowed us to speak honestly to one another and to explore possibilities for entering into a new or deeper understanding of the history, life and mission of the other tradition.

The group believes that the conclusions to these informal conversations should be shared and tested among the wider circles of the Church of England and Baptist Union of Great Britain constituencies. Within the report, at the end of key areas of discussion we suggest and identify questions for reflection and feedback. We hope that this report will be of interest not only to our parent bodies, but also to those with whom we are engaged in multilateral and bilateral conversations.

We have appreciated hearing of the progress of the international conversations between the Baptist World Alliance and the Anglican Communion which have taken place in parallel to these conversations.

We offer this report to the Church of England and the Baptist Union of Great Britain in the light of our shared ecumenical vision and our common membership of Churches Together in England, Churches Together in Britain and Ireland, the Conference of European Churches and the World Council of Churches. We are both sponsoring churches of Christian Aid and at local level Baptist and Church of England congregations are involved in over 175 Local

Ecumenical Partnerships and in Churches Together groups throughout the country. In the period of these conversations ecumenical dialogues have also significantly progressed for the Church of England with the Methodist Church of Great Britain and for the Baptist Union of Great Britain with the Independent Methodist Connexion.

As we have participated together in these informal conversations we have become very conscious of the opportunities which confront all the churches and the urgent need for unity for the sake of Christian mission. In the series of meetings whose discussions are reflected in this report, we have sought to explore together those things which unite us in a common expression and living out of the Christian faith and those areas of concern which still divide us.

We are conscious of the difficulties that have attended conversations between us in the past and of the diverse convictions which are held among us in both Christian traditions. There are unreconciled memories which need to go on being addressed, even as we have honestly sought in this round of conversations to face them together. The histories of our churches – notwithstanding notable examples of cooperation and conversation – have tended to develop in isolation from each other. Both traditions have sometimes been guilty of assuming spiritual superiority over the other. Now there is a strong desire amongst us to bridge the gap.

Since the nineteenth century we have both been involved in various para-church voluntary societies which, together with changes in our own structures and attitudes, help us now to talk with and understand each other. This report reflects those diversities, and demonstrates that we have treated with the utmost seriousness the situation in both our communions, but it nevertheless recognizes much that we have found to share and rejoice in together.

This report, then, explores common ground and differences and puts questions and challenges to Anglicans and Baptists. In several ways these conversations seem to have taken us beyond the strict limits of what is often thought to be possible in informal ecumenical conversations and we feel that we are 'pushing at the boundaries'. We encourage each church to promote the study and discussion of this report, both separately and together, and to monitor this process with a view to our considering together in due course what further steps on the road of Christian unity might become possible.

the historical
and ecumenical setting

chapter one

the historical context

our respective histories

The significance of the developing relationship between Baptists and Anglicans in England today can be understood only against the background of our respective histories. During the past four centuries a gap of mutual incomprehension and suspicion has existed between our two traditions. It is only hearing each other's stories and learning to understand each other's historical memories in today's rather different climate that can bridge this gap and provide a sound basis for a greater sharing in each other's life and mission.

At the time of the Reformation, the Church of England understood itself as the reformed embodiment of the catholic Church in England. It believed that it maintained the same faith, sacraments and ministry as the early Church. The claim of Elizabethan theologians was that the Church of England was both catholic and reformed. The Bishop of Rome was held to have no jurisdiction in the realm of England. The Pope subsequently excommunicated Queen Elizabeth I and called upon loyal Roman Catholics to oppose her rule. The involvement of lay people in the governance of the church, symbolized in the role of the monarch and Parliament, was justified on theological grounds. The existence of a vernacular Prayer Book (rather than a Latin liturgy), the Bible available in English, and Holy Communion administered in both kinds (bread and wine) testified to this concern for the participation of the laity in the life of the church. The Elizabethan Settlement aimed at a Christian comprehensiveness that was as wide as possible without jeopardizing the security of the realm. This concern is reflected in the Thirty-nine Articles of Religion, which sought to mark out the centre ground by ruling out unacceptable extremes. But the comprehensiveness was never complete. As well as those Roman Catholics (Recusants) who, unlike the 'church papists', refused outward conformity to the Church of England, there were other undercurrents of dissent.

Among these dissenters the Separatists established illegal autonomous congregations in the late sixteenth century. They sought the freedom to exist under the immediate rule of Christ and his word, rather than under any state-imposed rule of worship and discipline. The Separatists attempted to opt out of the territorial parochial structure of the Church of England in favour of gathered congregations that maintained rigorous discipline among themselves. What bound the true Church together, in their view, was the covenant between all of its members and the Lord.

The biblical concept of covenant was particularly important later for Baptists, who saw the Church of England of the seventeenth century as no longer participating in the covenant. Baptists typified restorationist traditions with their longing to return to the supposed biblical simplicity of the apostolic age. The Thirty-nine Articles of the Church of England explicitly condemn several Anabaptist tenets. However, there is a continuing debate among historians about the use of the term Anabaptist for the English Baptists, and about how far parts of the English Baptist tradition drew upon insights from the radical Reformation on the Continent. There is a widely held view that most English Baptist churches derived from the Separatist tradition of the late sixteenth century. Among the substantial dissenting communities that emerged in the seventeenth century were some who believed that the baptism of believers rather than of infants was a mark of Christ's disciples, bound as they were by covenant to him and to each other. The earliest congregation of General Baptists among English exiles from religious persecution at home emerged in Holland, with one group returning to England in 1611. The second main stream of Baptist life, the Calvinistic Particular Baptists, developed on English soil by the 1640s. They shared the same concern for congregational freedom within a pattern of interdependency and for believers' baptism as a sign of the covenant of God's grace.

Both of these Baptist groups belonged to that stream of spirituality that stressed the inner reality rather than the outward form. *The Book of Common Prayer* was viewed with suspicion by people who saw extempore prayer as a mark of sincerity and an expression of the inspiration of the Spirit. The Act of Uniformity of 1662 intensified their view of *The Book of Common Prayer* as an instrument of oppression, as many Baptists and other Nonconformists were fined or imprisoned. In return, many members of the Church of England viewed these dissenters with suspicion, regarding their delight in spontaneity and their avoidance of prescribed liturgical forms as anarchic and dismissive of the rich traditions of catholic spirituality.

Nevertheless Baptists and Anglicans eventually came to share a largely common hymnody. In recent decades, ecumenical engagement has broadened each tradition's awareness of the other's riches. Anglican liturgical forms have become more varied and Baptist worship leaders often use written and responsive prayers as resources alongside free prayer.

Today it is possible to recognize that both Anglican and Baptist traditions, in their different ways and in a period of reform and ferment, were seeking to acknowledge the rule of God in the world and to witness faithfully to the gospel of Christ. They were both looking for critical involvement with the world around them, a prophetic engagement in which any idolatrous claims of the state for ultimate authority could be challenged on behalf of the Lordship of Christ. However, for the two streams of church life, this stance took different forms: participation either in the established church or in dissenting communities. As each tradition developed, it produced certain emphases that we can now see should serve as a corrective to each other. Both, for example, recognized pastoral oversight in personal and communal forms, but while the Anglican tradition tended to look to the personal oversight of the bishop as a focus of unity, Baptists tended to emphasize the authority exercised by the whole Christian community (gathered in Church Meeting and Association) as it sought the mind of Christ.

By the early nineteenth century both Anglicans and Baptists had been influenced by the Evangelical Revival and, with others, were working in many evangelical voluntary societies which transcended denominational barriers (Sunday Schools, prison reform, abolition of slavery, Bible translation, etc.). In contrast, the Oxford Movement, which was viewed with deep suspicion by Baptists, accentuated differences. The reaction against it especially affected Baptist understanding of the Lord's Supper and popular memory of this lingers among Baptists today. The long struggle for full civil rights ensured that Nonconformists opposed the establishment of the Church of England by law: exclusion from these rights provoked a radical response. Rivalry between the British and Foreign School Society and the Anglican National Society delayed a national system of primary education, while university education in England was closed to dissenters until the founding of University College London. Nonconformists objected to being required to use Anglican birth and marriage registration and burial rites, and resented compulsory church rates. Many were active in the Anti-State Church Association/Liberation Society.

Wider political issues also divided Baptists and Anglicans. English Baptists had generally supported the American Revolution, while English Anglicans generally supported those Americans who remained loyal to the Crown. As the franchise was widened and Nonconformists became more active politically, Baptists and Anglicans were often on different sides, so conflict between Liberals and Tories added to tensions stirred by the 'Nonconformist Conscience', resulting in controversies like those over church schools, trade unions and aspects of the Boer War.

Yet there was also increasing goodwill between different branches of the Christian Church, to which the Lambeth Quadrilateral of 1888 bore witness. The Baptist Union Assembly in 1889 welcomed the growing desire for unity manifested by this approach and endorsed the first of the four Articles (on the Holy Scriptures), but felt that the terms of the other three were still so ambiguous as to make a profitable outcome to any deliberations based on them unlikely. The *Appeal to All Christian People*, issued by the Lambeth Conference of 1920, marked a further development in relationships between the Church of England and the Baptist Union of Great Britain. The Baptist reply to the Lambeth Appeal was adopted by the Annual Assembly in 1926. Though the Appeal for other churches to accept the historic episcopate as part of the basis for reunion was rejected by Baptists, they expressed a desire to strengthen contacts and links in order that 'unity may be displayed to the world'.

It was leaders in the missionary movements within many churches who saw clearly that the divisions between the churches hindered the mission of the Church, making the gospel of reconciliation less than credible. At the International Missionary Conference at Edinburgh in 1910, Bishop Charles Brent (an American Episcopalian) was convinced of the importance of seeking full doctrinal agreement if divided churches were to come together. His vision led to the First World Conference on Faith and Order at Lausanne in 1927, to which both Baptists and Anglicans sent representatives. These two streams of the ecumenical movement (the International Missionary Council, and Faith and Order) were eventually brought together with Life and Work in the formation of the World Council of Churches in 1948. Anglicans and Baptists have worked, and continue to work, closely together within the World Council of Churches, the Conference of European Churches and the ecumenical bodies in this country. Both of our communions are influenced by the emerging ecumenical convergence and consensus expressed in multilateral and bilateral dialogues. In this century we have increasingly shared biblical and historical scholarship – Anglicans contributing particularly to New Testament studies, Baptists to Old Testament studies. Students for the ordained ministry from both traditions have studied together in English universities and increasingly do so in consortia of theological colleges. Both the Church of England and the Baptist Union of Great Britain have been undergoing far-reaching changes. Both are affected by the same ecumenical currents and insights, though they do not always react to these in the same way.

Anglican–Baptist dialogue

At various times in the past century there have been exchanges of letters or informal meetings between representatives of the Baptist Union of Great Britain and of the Church of England. Following *The Appeal to all Christian People* issued by the Lambeth Conference in 1920, the Baptist Union participated with other Free Churches in conversations with the Church of England that were temporarily suspended in 1925. A second series of Anglican–Free Church conversations, which took place during the 1930s, was aborted because of the Second World War.

In 1946 the then Archbishop of Canterbury, Geoffrey Fisher, invited the Free Churches to take episcopacy into their own systems and to try it out on their own ground as a stage towards communion with the Church of England. The Baptist Union Council replied to this call in 1953, but rejected making inter-communion dependent on episcopacy. The opening of Holy Communion in the Church of England to baptized communicants in good standing in other churches during the 1970s contributed to a significant improvement in relations between Baptists and Anglicans.

The Church of England and the Baptist Union of Great Britain had already been involved in the formation of the British Council of

Churches and both joined the World Council of Churches at its inception. More recently, both shared in the Inter-Church Process and in the formation of Churches Together in England and the Council of Churches for Britain and Ireland (later Churches Together in Britain and Ireland). In all these various bodies Baptist and Church of England representatives have cooperated together and taken opportunities to keep in touch with developments within the other tradition.

At least four meetings were held in the 1980s between representatives of the Church of England and of the Baptist Union of Great Britain to discuss issues arising out of the WCC Faith and Order Commission's report *Baptism, Eucharist and Ministry*. In 1992 discussions were opened between the Church of England's Council for Christian Unity and the Faith and Unity Executive of the Baptist Union of Great Britain to see whether the time was appropriate for what was then envisaged as a one-off informal meeting to discuss items of mutual concern. Such a meeting was convened at Regent's Park College, Oxford, in December 1992 and further meetings have generally been held twice a year since then.

chapter two

Anglican–Baptist relations: encouragement from the past

The seventeenth century saw the development of the three main branches of Old Dissent in Presbyterian, Independent (Congregational) and Baptist forms. When this happened some people maintained older friendships while others separated with more ill feeling. The politics of the Stuart era did little to sweeten relationships, with Stuart Anglicans and Cromwellian Nonconformists persecuting each other by turns, but the level of persecution varied considerably, according to the whim of local magistrates.[1] Some Christians with differing convictions may have held one another in respect and even friendship, but records are thin, and outrage at persecution was more likely to be recorded than unfashionably good relationships. After the Glorious Revolution, which brought William and Mary to the throne in 1688, and the 1689 Act of Toleration, friendlier accounts began to appear. Nonconformists could now obtain a 'bishop's licence' for a meeting house, provided they assented to all but three, or for Baptists four, of the Thirty-nine Articles (XXXIV, XXXV, XXXVI, and XXVII).

At Abingdon, near Oxford, in an area at the heart of the Civil War, tension between Nonconformists and the two Anglican churches was inevitable and severe. Yet in 1699 and 1704 Presbyterians and Baptists joined with St Helen's to raise money for Protestants in Orange in the South of France, where Huguenots had found refuge until Louis XIV seized the princedom from William III of Orange. The record does not give the first amount collected but the churchwardens paid 2s 6d for its safe carriage to Oxford. In 1704 Anglicans contributed £9 18s 3d, Baptists £7 10s 9d, and Presbyterians £18 15s 6d. Fresh from persecuting one another, they could find common cause.[2]

William Grimshaw, vicar of Haworth (d.1763), was influential in West Yorkshire, not least on the Baptist revival there. William

Crabtree, first minister of Westgate Baptist Church, Bradford, was converted under Grimshaw, and the young John Fawcett often went to hear Grimshaw preach. A few years later John Fawcett and Dan Taylor, neighbouring Baptist ministers in Calderdale, were joined in Bible study by the Anglican ordinand Henry Foster, a student of The Queen's College, Oxford. According to William Underwood's *Life of Dan Taylor* (1870), the three read the classics, studied divinity and cultivated other branches of knowledge together. Taylor moved to London in 1785 and Foster, by then a popular preacher and lecturer there, renewed personal contact with him.[3] At a time when many parish churches languished without regular leadership, converts of evangelicals like Grimshaw often found a later home among Baptists. Thus the Church Book of the Baptists of Walgrave, Northamptonshire, records in July 1785,

> On the 17th of this month about 6 o'clock in the Lord's Day morning died in the 73rd year of his age the Revd Abraham Maddock, curate of Creton. He was a faithful ambassador of the Prince of Peace, had an affectionate desire for the salvation of sinners, preached the free invitation of the Gospel to them. God owned his labours. His ministry laid the foundation for the raising the Baptist church at Gillsbro [Gilsborough]. Some that attended his ministry found the Baptist church at Clipstone; and others the Baptist church at Walgrave. Mr Maddock in his pleasant hours used to say of his congregation, though we have swarmed and cast, yet blessed be God we continue full. This is mentioned to perpetuate the memory of a useful minister.[4]

Evangelical Anglicans were often on excellent terms with their Baptist neighbours. This was particularly striking at Olney in Buckinghamshire. When John Newton went to the parish church in 1764 he quickly sought fellowship with the local Baptist and Congregational ministers. He met the redoubtable Baptist, John Collet Ryland, in February 1765; they had previously corresponded on matters of High Calvinist doctrine. Ryland later described Newton as one of his most helpful mentors. In 1763 Newton visited Olney Baptist Church to hear a sermon by William Grant, Baptist pastor at Wellingborough. Newton commented, 'A more excellent sermon I never heard.' When Newton's friend Samuel Brewer, a Congregational minister, visited at Christmas 1765, he preached at both the Congregational and Baptist churches with Newton in attendance. Afterwards, Newton invited John Drake, the Congregational minister, and William Walker, the Baptist pastor, to join them for tea at the vicarage. During 1777–8 the three churches inaugurated annual services for young people, one in each church on successive evenings around New Year. When the Northamptonshire Baptist Association held its annual meetings in Olney in 1776, both Newton and William Cowper attended, Newton particularly praising the preaching of Abraham Booth. As the Baptist chapel was small, the meetings were held in the open air, using the orchard behind Cowper's garden and Newton's vicarage. Newton preached on the third day on a text from Zechariah.

When John Sutcliff was ordained to the Baptist ministry at Olney, Newton found Caleb Evans's sermon 'sensible and solid'. John Fawcett was also present and noted Sutcliff's friendship with Newton with approval. In January 1776 Newton altered the timing of his service so that adults too could hear Sutcliff preach at the youth service. Later Sutcliff befriended Newton's successors. Newton's influence on Baptists was not just local: when without a preacher, the Baptists of Whitchurch in Hampshire, for example, used to read aloud Newton's sermons. They wrote to tell him of this, hoping that one day he might preach to them in person.[5]

In 1790 or 1791 Sutcliff and Andrew Fuller of Kettering, both influential Baptist ministers, visited an aged Anglican evangelical, John Berridge, whom Sutcliff subsequently described in glowing terms. At Thomas Morgan's ordination, Sutcliff said, 'Cheerfully we own that the Established Church is honoured with a noble list of worthies. Their names we love. Their memories we revere.' Elsewhere Sutcliff wrote of his commitment to evangelicals of other denominations:

> While we perceive not only varieties, but contrarieties in the views and feelings even of eminent Christians, the former are but as the various features, and the latter as the accidental spots, in the human countenance. The great and essential principles of Christianity are found in every Christian, no less than the distinguishing properties of humanity are found in every man.[6]

The younger John Ryland, another prominent Baptist minister, had close friendships with a number of evangelical Anglicans, including Augustus Toplady (a High Calvinist), and the Bible commentator Thomas Scott. Robert Hall, a Baptist who was in his day perhaps the best-known English preacher and who had keen political interests, preached in Bristol in 1820 in aid of the National Society, although the education this promoted was expressly Anglican. His address, 'The Signs of the Times', was a plea for Christian unity. Another extended sermon of Hall's, on 'Modern Infidelity', prompted warm appreciation and a gift of books from Bishop Porteous of London. Dr William Mansel, Master of Trinity College, Cambridge, and Bishop of Bristol, tried to persuade Hall to join the Church of England.

By the early nineteenth century evangelicals from both Anglican and Free Churches were joining in a variety of common causes: the Sunday School movement, Bible translation, and various bodies addressing social concerns. These drew both ministers and laypeople; many friendships must have resulted. William Wilberforce was in close contact with Baptists over slavery and, with other Anglicans, supported the infant Baptist Missionary Society, the first such society in Britain. Jamaican missionaries of the Baptist Missionary Society were ardent anti-slavery campaigners. As various new Protestant missionary societies got under way, they gladly agreed to allocate particular areas to different denominational work rather than to compete. William Carey, the first Baptist missionary, wrote from India to a friend in 1813, 'The cause of truth in India has lately suffered a heavy loss in the death of Mr Martyn, a very amiable and pious clergyman of the Church of England . . . We have however two other very useful ministers of the Church of England at this Residency, Viz. Mr Corrie and Mr Thomason and one at Madras – Mr Thompson.'[7]

Joseph Hughes, Baptist minister in Battersea and first secretary of the British and Foreign Bible Society, valued his friendship with members of the Clapham Sect. His ecumenical vision was not limited to educational and philanthropic activities: 'I long to see the day in which Episcopalians, Presbyterians, Methodists, Independents, and Baptists will exchange pulpits, and meet at the same sacramental board.'[8]

Baptists supported Lord Shaftesbury's Ragged School movement. It was Shaftesbury who dubbed Bloomsbury Chapel's domestic missionary to the nearby slums, George M'Cree, 'the Bishop of St Giles'. Shaftesbury acted as mediator when Baptists had a major disagreement with the Bible Society. The Refuges associated with the St Giles' and St George's Ragged Schools, sent girls to worship at St Giles church, but boys to the Baptist Chapel.

In the 1840s the reforming Bishop of Norwich, Edward Stanley, and the Dean of Ely were both impressed with the Christian care shown to navvies by the Baptist railway contractor Morton Peto. Bishop Stanley was also friendly with William Brock, Baptist minister in Norwich. In 1841 the Bishop sent Brock a copy of Archdeacon Hare's work *The Victory of Faith* (1840). The Archdeacon, former tutor, friend and brother-in-law of F. D. Maurice, was also a lifelong friend of Sir Henry Havelock, the Baptist military hero. The Bishop was delighted with the subsequent exchange between Brock and Hare, observing, 'If all Christians differed and discussed their differences in his and your temper, we might hope for a wider diffusion of Christian spirit than now prevails amongst the controversial leaders of the religious world.'

Brock supported the Liberation Society's disestablishment campaign, and nearly went to prison for opposing the *compulsory* church rate (he was prepared to encourage the dissenting majority in his home parish to make an equal *voluntary* contribution), but these stands on matters of principle did not spoil his friendships with Anglican neighbours. In similar vein, William Bailey, Baptist minister in Datchet 1819–44, 'was on such good terms with the vicar of St Mary's, the Rev. Isaac Gossett, that when Datchet Baptists were building their own first place of worship, the vicar gave £2 towards the cost'.[9]

Anglican reformers seem to have been welcomed by those Baptists with a heart for the wider Church – and respect was not limited to evangelicals. Brock and John Clifford, for example, both admired Dr Arnold of Rugby. Clifford described him as the 'herald of religion in common life', while Brock defended Arnold against charges of being unevangelical and unspiritual in a letter to Sir Morton Peto's wife: 'The truth is, Arnold had a strong aversion to the Evangelicals on account of their narrow-mindedness and sanctimoniousness . . . these two horrid things.' When Brock went to London in 1848 as first minister of Bloomsbury Chapel, he used to walk down Gower Street on Sunday mornings with the Rector of St George's, Bloomsbury, the Revd the Hon. Henry Montagu Villiers, later Bishop of Durham. They would exchange a blessing as they parted for their respective churches. Both had a keen concern for the poor and were glad to see other Christians addressing the pressing needs of the district.[10]

The Evangelical Alliance included both Anglicans and Baptists, and dared to experiment with communion services open to all members – which must have disturbed some Anglicans and deterred strict-communion Baptists. The Alliance was formed in 1846; the most famous communion service in the early years was at a conference in Paris in 1855, with 1,200 people attending.[11] After that, shared communion seems to have been practised quite often, mainly at large international events.

Baptists' deep unease at the rise of Anglo-Catholicism coloured their attitude to the Church of England. Meanwhile, members of the Free Churches gradually gained full rights as citizens, and Victorian Baptists were almost all keen political supporters of the Anglican Gladstone. Numbers of Baptist children bore his name. For many Baptists it could be said, as of George M'Cree, that their politics could be summed up in three words, 'William Ewart Gladstone'. Clearly his churchmanship was not a problem for Baptists.

In the twentieth century recognition of the Free Churches as part of the legitimate and diverse church life of Britain made relationships easier, but that in turn made the sticking points of difference more painful. Church records tend to highlight relations between clergy, but each ministerial friendship could probably be matched by several unrecorded friendships between lay Christians from different church traditions glad to share their faith in workplace or home. In a sense, all these are summed up in remembering those between their leaders: as when Archbishop Runcie, pursued by journalists after a provocative statement, called on his old colleague from St Albans at Bristol Baptist College. Principal Morris West slammed the great oak door in the faces of the newshounds and told the archbishop, 'It's all right. You're amongst friends here.'[12]

In the middle of the twentieth century many Baptists were encouraged towards ecumenical endeavour by Ernest Payne, General Secretary of the Baptist Union and a President of the World Council of Churches. He planned his own memorial service to be held at the Bloomsbury church, but at the request of the Dean of Westminster it was transferred to the Abbey. For those Baptists present on 27 February 1980 who were aware of their history – and few had studied it more keenly than Dr Payne – it was strangely moving to leave with the Abbey bells ringing out in tribute to a great Baptist ecumenist and unrepentant advocate of Free Churches.

chapter three

Anglicans and Baptists in Local Ecumenical Partnerships

introduction

Local Ecumenical Partnerships (LEPs) are now widespread in England, and many include both Baptists and Anglicans, alongside United Reformed Church members, Methodists, Moravians, Roman Catholics and other smaller denominations in varying combinations. There are some which are a single congregation, meeting in common for all aspects of church life. Others are congregations in covenanted partnerships embracing a number of locations, or shared church partnerships, where two or more separate congregations share a single church building. Some are intentional LEPs from the outset, while others consist of churches which have developed sufficiently close fellowship to enter into covenant together. For instance, the Church of Christ the Cornerstone in central Milton Keynes embraces five denominations, and was intentionally developed as an ecumenical church, while Grange Park Church, Northampton, is a Church of England–Baptist LEP, planted by Baptists in a new housing development on the edge of Northampton, and joined soon afterwards by parishioners from a Church of England parish in the town centre. Trinity Baptist Church in Chesham is in covenant relationship with the Church of England parish and the Methodist and United Reformed Church churches in the town, but does not share a building with any of them, while Wendover Free Church is a Baptist–United Reformed Church congregation which shares its buildings with the Roman Catholic parish and has a covenanted relationship with the Church of England parish church.

In September 2003, of the 852 LEPs in England, 228 involved Baptist churches and 612 involved Anglicans. There were 175 LEPs which involved both Church of England and Baptist churches, and of these 13 involved only Anglicans and Baptists (9 were single congregation, type 1, Baptist–Anglican LEPs). It is clear that the geographical distribution is varied, with some Associations having as few as 6 LEPs (4 per cent of the member churches in the South East Baptist Partnership, with one of its counties, Kent, having none) or 2 (2 per cent of churches in the South West Baptist Association) while Central has the highest proportion and number, 21 churches (13 per cent of the churches, with 15 LEPs involving Anglicans, 71 per cent of its LEPs). In some areas there is more involvement of Free Churches than Anglicans (Yorkshire Baptist Association has 14 LEPs, with only 6 involving Anglicans, 43 per cent) while elsewhere Anglican–Baptist LEPs predominate (66 per cent of the Heart of England LEPs include Anglicans).

The presence of churches with such differing polities as Baptist and Anglican, with baptismal policies that are similarly varied, cohabiting in the same local fellowship or congregation raises significant pastoral questions:

1 How are children to be regarded within the fellowship, especially in relation to the Eucharist?

2 How does the authority of the Church Meeting relate to the authority of the bishop and the synodical structures of the Church of England? What are the implications of establishment for Church of England parishes which are in LEPs?

3 How are new clergy appointed, and what is the interplay between local call and denominational appointment?

4 How do we recognize the growing numbers of men and women in LEPs who do not wish to be categorized as either Baptist or Anglican, but wish to be considered simply as members of such-and-such ecumenical church? What happens when such people move house?

There are, of course, general ecumenical protocols to be followed, but new situations arise often, especially in a post-denominational age.

an example from Milton Keynes

In Milton Keynes these questions are raised in at least two forums: the local LEP and the shared oversight group, the Presidents' Meeting, comprising the Church of England Bishop of Buckingham, Baptist Senior Regional Minister (Central Baptist Association), Methodist Thames North-West District Chair, United Reformed Church East Midlands Synod Moderator and the Roman Catholic Bishop of Northampton. This group also includes the Milton Keynes Ecumenical Moderator. In this group, precedence is not afforded to any one tradition, all have equal responsibilities towards the Mission Partnership (previously the Milton Keynes Council of Churches), and all equally share the funding of the Ecumenical Moderator. The chair is a revolving one-year appointment between the five denominational leaders. Issues such as the place of children at communion are debated by this group and their decision is recommended to the Assembly of the churches for action. In this way shared oversight is given practical expression.

The Presidents' Group uses consensus as its modus operandi and relies heavily upon the quality of the relationships of the individual church leaders occupying the various roles of *episkope*, within the limits of canon law and denominational practice. In particular, the responsibilities that cannot be delegated by the Church of England bishop (such as confirmations), and the limits of authority exercised by the Baptist regional minister in the context of congregational government, both place limitations upon the degree of ecumenical overlap.

In general, any decision reached in response to pastoral issues seeks to accommodate the concerns of all. For instance, faced with some LEPs requesting that children be admitted to Communion, the decision was taken not to approve such practice, even though the pressure to admit came from more than one tradition (Anglican and Baptist). This was out of a concern that decisions should not be made which then excluded other already existing participants.

One of the interesting outcomes of those situations where the LEP is joint Anglican and Baptist is a readiness to value aspects of both traditions that are often weaker in single denomination churches. So the place of congregational decision-making is stronger than it might otherwise be in a Church of England parish (with a regular

Church Meeting held), while the influence of the regional minister is stronger than in stand-alone Baptist churches, being institutionalized and structured in a way that ensures influence, as opposed to the option where consultation with a regional minister is by choice.

pastoral oversight

At the level of wider oversight in ecumenical settings, two groups emerge as having significance in offering appropriate *episkope*. County Ecumenical Committees supply the more technical and legal oversight, often with a body in which the properties of shared churches are vested. In the Diocese of St Albans, for instance, the LEPs which share property, such as Grove Hill Church, Hemel Hempstead, occupy buildings owned by Hertfordshire Shared Churches Ltd. Representatives of the denominations involved act as directors and trustees, including senior church leaders such as a Church of England bishop and the Baptist regional minister. Their task is not merely that of supervising property, but also of monitoring the health of the congregations using the buildings.

Less 'hands-on', but perhaps more influential, are the Church Leaders' groups involved. Generally organized around the Church of England diocesan structures or, where a diocese is not coterminous with a county, at county level (ignoring some Unitary Authorities as far too recent an innovation), these groups always include Church of England bishops, Roman Catholic bishops, chairs of Methodist districts, United Reformed Church synod moderators and Baptist regional ministers; and they usually include Salvation Army divisional commanders. A few include Orthodox metropolitans, Pentecostal leaders and new church apostles, but these are the exceptions.

It is in these peer group settings that ecumenical thinking takes place, new and strategic opportunities are discussed and, more generally, peer support is offered to those who share in the oversight of the churches, ecumenical or otherwise. While a few still maintain an air of deference to Anglican superiority, at their best these are genuine peer groups. For instance, a recent 'Herts and Beds' Church Leaders' group discussed, amongst other matters, a new church plant near Bedford, difficulties faced in locally recognized ministry, the Catholic Westminster Diocesan

Mission, a recent visit to Brussels, and the Conference of European Churches. As a group with no fixed agenda, it was able to respond to current issues, new initiatives and perennial challenges in a mutually supportive way.

These groups are not formally expressions of shared *episkope*, but to a limited extent they are practically so, and in the case of the Milton Keynes Mission Partnership, actually so. Whether the Milton Keynes experiment is a blueprint for wider expressions of shared *episkope* remains to be seen, although it has rich potential to act as a model for elsewhere. The failure of a project to reach agreement on an ecumenical bishop for Cardiff does not offer hope of any immediate enthusiasm for such development, but as many of the historic families of churches face either stagnation or decline in membership, vocations and incomes, the benefits of ecumenical cooperation may point a way forward for a reversal of this trend, adding financial advantages to the benefits of closer fellowship and more effective witness in a challenging cultural context.

shared local life in worship and witness

The character of ecumenical cooperation in an LEP differs widely. Where there is shared worship this might be either more formal in its liturgy, reflecting a greater influence of Anglican liturgical practice than would be usual in a Baptist church, or more informal or charismatic, reflecting those trends in both denominations which have significantly reshaped liturgical practice over the past twenty-five years. It would not be true to say that LEPs are uniformly more structured in worship than other Baptist churches or less so than most Church of England parishes, although the suspicions amongst their detractors suggest so. In truth, there is great variety, and often a richness in the worship which is greater than would be possible in single denomination congregations. If it is true that in a post-denominational age the Sunday morning service is the shop window of the church for a consumer culture, then the quality and attractiveness of the liturgy is perhaps the most significant factor for those shopping for a new church. Ecumenical worship which is not the lowest common denominator, but the result of great variety and riches of resourcing, involving both the framework of a structured liturgy and the spontaneity of more contemporary modes, has the possibility of being amongst the most attractive to the consumer generation (however fervently we might deplore this aspect of our contemporary culture on ethical or philosophical grounds).

In the more highly developed LEPs there is the possibility of a shared Eucharist, and of a baptismal policy that enables the Church of England minister to offer either baptism of infants or a service of 'Thanksgiving for the Gift of a Child'. However, where a Baptist minister presides at the Eucharist, this remains a Baptist communion service, and if the LEP is also the only Church of England parish church in the parish, the Eucharist presided at by an Anglican priest is still required on certain holy days. Currently, the ability of a Baptist minister to offer the baptism of infants in a single-minister LEP where he or she is in pastoral charge is limited. The vexed issue of lay presidency at the Eucharist calls for particular sensitivity. This is permissible in Baptist churches, but unknown in Anglican churches. A celebration of the Eucharist presided over by a Baptist lay person is always a Baptist communion, just as one presided over by a Baptist minister is always a Baptist communion. There is a particular need to ensure that careful attention is drawn to the manner in which such lay people are appointed to the task by the Church Meeting.

Joint confirmation services where a Church of England bishop and the Baptist regional minister, together with appropriate ministers of other participating denominations, take part in the laying on of hands are now common. Unless multiple membership is being offered to the candidate, it is generally clear, however, that this remains a confirmation service of Church of England members, with confirmation presided over by their bishop, notwithstanding a generous welcome to other church leaders to participate in it.

convergence

One of the processes at work in ecumenical cooperation is an awareness of the degree to which some processes seem remarkably similar, even when they arise from different ecclesiological roots. Take the appointment of clergy and ministers, for instance. In Baptist churches, the responsibility for a call to the pastorate lies with the local congregational meeting. Candidates are commended by a National Settlement Team (comprising regional ministers who carry settlement responsibilities), which attempts to match potential candidates for the pastorate of any given church to its expectations and churchmanship, but the decision to call lies not with the regional minister who exercises *episkope*, but the local church. The only constraint upon the choice of minister involves those churches whose trust deeds require that the pastor be an accredited Baptist minister. Here the national structures of ministerial recognition impinge more obviously upon the autonomy of the local church, although in practice most Baptist churches will appoint an accredited Baptist minister to their pastorate if finances allow.

In a Church of England parish, parochial posts are often advertised in the church press, or a parish may call for candidates from its archdeacon. It is the patron who offers the living where the post is a freehold (i.e. tenured) vicar or rector, although the parish representatives have influence by virtue of their right of appeal to the bishop. There is usually wide consultation in the parish, and occasionally ecumenically. A priest-in-charge is appointed by the bishop, and will have no freehold of the living, but a similar level of consultation in the parish will usually apply. However, all parish clergy, whether in possession of a freehold living or not, must be licensed by the bishop. The two different processes are remarkably similar in some respects, such as breadth of consultation and requests for nominations.

Here are two different processes with a common aim – to discern the will of God in the call of a minister to the pastoral leadership of a local church – and the prayerful approach by all concerned, albeit with differing responsibilities and levels of authority, produces remarkably similar results. Both Church of England bishops and Baptist regional ministers have responsibilities for the discipline and care of clergy and other officers, and both work best when oversight is welcomed by the clergy and people, and offered in humility and with consultation.

The reality on the ground is of far more similarities than differences between Church of England parish life and a local Baptist congregation, which is not to minimize the outstanding theological differences in areas of apostolicity, baptism, Eucharist and ministry.

the practice of church life in Local Ecumenical Partnerships

Returning now to the opening questions, the following addresses some of the acute points of discussion around the practice of church life in LEPs.

1 How are children to be regarded within the fellowship, especially in relation to the Eucharist?

The impetus for the admission of children to the Eucharist comes from a variety of sources. There are those who want to be as inclusive of children as possible, and see no overwhelming reason why eucharistic participation should not precede either confirmation or believers' baptism. Many emphasize the importance of belonging to the fellowship of the church from infancy. Traditionally, first communion follows confirmation in Anglican settings, and baptism in Baptist. Therefore the solution in many places at present is to discourage the practice of children taking the elements prior to confirmation or baptism.

2 How does the authority of the Church Meeting relate to the authority of the bishop and the synodical structures of the Church of England? What are the implications of establishment for Church of England parishes which are in LEPs?

The Church Meeting should include all who are members of the congregation, not just Baptists, and this allows all who are on both the Baptist and Church of England rolls to participate. However, where authority for particular matters lies within the remit of synodical structures for the Anglicans, this might enable the wisdom of the wider Christian community to be sought, and thus enrich the Baptist Church Meeting with that wider perspective. Careful understanding of what does and does not lie within the remit of the Church Meeting needs to be agreed at the outset.

3 How are new clergy appointed, and what is the interplay between local call and denominational appointment?

Intermediate bodies need to have an agreed procedure for the search for and appointment of new ministry. In one Church of

England–Baptist–Methodist–United Reformed Church LEP with a recent pastoral vacancy, a search group was established, representing all the constituent denominations, and charged with a search by advertisement or nomination. The search group short-listed applicants for the post, which was open to an ordained minister of any of the four denominations. The group was local in personnel but appointed regionally, expressing both the local and wider denominational components. The Church of England bishop encouraged an Anglican to apply, just as the Baptist regional minister nominated a couple of Baptists from the national Settlement List. The search group, appointed by the intermediate body, acted as the patron, in Church of England terms, and as the diaconate, in Baptist terms. Good practice is described in *Travelling Together*, by Elizabeth Welch and Flora Winfield, second edition, Churches Together in England, 2004.

4 How do we recognize the growing numbers of men and women in LEPs who do not wish to be categorized as either Baptist or Anglican, but wish to be considered simply as members of such-and-such ecumenical church? What happens when such people move?

The practice of multiple membership is now well established. This allows for a person newly coming to faith within an LEP to be baptized, confirmed and received into full membership of all the participating denominations at the same time. Extended membership is a similar concept, and allows someone already in membership of one of the denominations within an LEP to extend that membership to other denominations participating. In both cases, the extended membership applies only while persons holding it attend the LEP. If or when they move to a different church, their membership reverts to whichever denomination they were originally, or, in the case of those with multiple membership, they choose with which denomination they would like to remain in membership.

The concepts of multiple and extended membership go some way towards recognizing those who do not wish to be categorized denominationally, while still keeping to the legal requirement of holding denominational lists of members – multiple and extended members are simply recorded on each list, and church statistics are adjusted accordingly.

In many respects this problem of denominational identity is not confined to LEPs. Many, when they move, will seek a new church, not primarily on grounds of previous denominational affiliation so much as the style of worship, the welcome received and the provision of children's and youth work.

one baptism? towards a common understanding

chapter four

one baptism:
a Baptist contribution

problems with 'common baptism'

Baptists have not often used the historic creeds of the Christian
Church in their worship, preferring to appeal directly to Scripture
as primary witness to the revelation of God in Jesus Christ. Many
Baptist church members will thus be unfamiliar with the affirmation
in the Creed of Nicaea-Constantinople, 'We believe in . . . one
baptism for the forgiveness of sins.' They are, however, well aware
of the scriptural declaration in Ephesians 4.5, 'One Lord, one faith,
one baptism', which is one source (along with Acts 2.38) for the
line in the creed. Some will know the phrase from Ephesians as
part of the logo for the Baptist World Alliance. It may seem ironic,
then, that Baptists have been reluctant to accept the widespread
idea that all Christian people share a 'common baptism'. The
conviction that 'through our common baptism we are all brought
into Christ, and this forms the basis of our ecumenical engagement
with each other'[1] has become an accepted departure point in
relations between Christian churches, and it may seem wilfully
obstructive for Baptist churches to be doubtful about whether one
can in fact speak so easily of a common baptism at the present
stage of the history of the Christian Church.

The Baptist position is based on making a distinction, explicitly or
implicitly, between the 'one baptism' of the New Testament witness
and so-called 'common baptism'. To understand that distinction,
and to take it seriously, may make it possible to move towards a
mutual recognition of baptismal practices, and a formal recognition
of each other as communities of the apostolic faith, in a way that
will not be achieved by using the two phrases interchangeably.
Baptist resistance to the phrase 'common baptism' rests on its
implication that the present baptismal practices of the Christian
Church are simply equivalent to each other; in particular, it implies
that the baptism of a believer is exactly the same event as the
baptism of a very young infant. This impression is underlined by
the development on the British scene of a Common Baptismal

Certificate. Baptists are very diverse in their understanding of the meaning of baptism, but there is at least this agreement between them: that the baptism of believers, bearing witness to their own faith, has substantial differences from the baptism of very young children. Whether there can be said, from a Baptist point of view, to be an underlying continuity between the two events, so that they can be recognized as the same kind of event, is something that this paper intends to explore. But to identify the theological truth of 'one baptism' with a 'common baptism' seems to Baptists to short-circuit the whole discussion. Outside the specialist area of theological debate, it will give rise to some disappointment and frustration in church relations if we underestimate the instinctive feeling among Baptist congregations that believers' baptism and infant baptism are not the same thing.

It is important, moreover, to make clear, right at the beginning, that the difference between the two events is not only the opportunity for the exercise of human faith in response to God's offer of salvation, though this may often seem to be the characteristic Baptist emphasis. The very term 'believers' baptism' stresses the Baptist conviction that persons coming to the waters of baptism should be able to turn away from human sinfulness and confess their faith in Christ for themselves (Acts 2.38; 8.37). But the baptism of a disciple, involving commissioning for service in the world, is also a place for the activity of God's grace in a way that Baptists find hard to see happening in the case of very young infants. Another way of putting this agreed view among Baptists would be to say that the meaning contained in the symbolism of baptism, as portrayed in the New Testament, can be given *best* expression and actualization in the baptism of a believer. The baptismal pool may be pictured as a meeting-place between the believer and the triune God. Emil Brunner envisaged baptism as a place of 'divine–human encounter', a 'two-sided happening' involving 'personal correspondence'.[2] This personal meeting is, of course, never private but always in the context of the community; it is in the company of others that believers come to meet God – Father, Son and Holy Spirit – with their trusting love, however weak it is. God meets them in everlasting love, to transform their lives. The New Testament thus speaks of this meeting with a profusion of pictures of God's grace; it is a moment of new birth (John 3.5; Titus 3.5), forgiveness and cleansing from sin (Acts 2.38; 1 Corinthians 6.11, Hebrews 10.22), participation in the death, burial and resurrection of Christ (Romans 6.1-11;

Colossians 2.11,12; 1 Peter 3.21), immersion in the Holy Spirit and the receiving of spiritual gifts (1 Corinthians 12.13; Acts 2.38; 10.47), deliverance from evil powers (Colossians 1.13), union with Christ (Galatians 3.27), adoption as a child of God (Galatians 3.26), and membership in the body of Christ (1 Corinthians 12.13; Galatians 3.27-28).[3]

The London Confession of Particular Baptists in 1644 states that baptism by immersion 'being a signe, must answer the thing signified'.[4] While Baptist confessions such as this have been anxious not to confuse the 'sign' with the 'thing signified', they do look for some real correspondence and connection ('answer') between the two. Baptists in the present day differ about the nature of this connection; there is a diversity of views about the extent to which the rich symbolism of baptism is effective as well as expressive in operation. Baptists are not agreed about whether the transforming grace of God is communicated as well as portrayed in baptism, or in what sense. But they are agreed that the baptism of infants does not have the same scope for the rich symbolism of baptism to be displayed. Baptists will not want to deny that aspects of the grace of God and the faith of believers can be found in the act of sprinkling or immersing infants in water. But in so far as they find it difficult to locate all the benefits of baptism in the life of a very young infant, the notion of 'common baptism' is problematic.

It has been said, in classic Anglican formulations, that the baptism of a child is a sign of the promise of God. In this way of thinking, the gift of salvation is already fully bestowed, as far as God is concerned, in the event of baptism itself; but this gift is also a promise that will be increasingly fulfilled as the child appropriates for himself or herself what has been given, even as the human promises of the parents and sponsors are later assumed and renewed by the one who was baptized. Baptists will also, of course, expect there to be an overplus of promise in the event of baptism, an openness of promise which will be given fulfilment in the future in new and surprising ways. But because the person baptized is appropriating through his or her own faith what God is giving in salvation, Baptists will think that there is a kind of fulfilment of divine promise in the baptism of a believer which is not present in the baptism of a young child. This, then, is another reason why there is a difficulty in equating infant baptism with the baptism of a believing disciple. Baptists will want to suggest, moreover, that this difficulty does not only stand between Baptists and Anglicans. There is surely a theological issue here for Anglicans, who practise both kinds of baptism under the same name.

the scriptural meaning of 'one baptism'

If Baptists find problems with the idea of 'common baptism', what do they mean by 'one baptism'? Baptists will come to a passage like Ephesians 4.4-6 with different presuppositions from those who practise infant baptism and these need teasing out. Baptist readers will assume that the author of this passage (who was either the Apostle Paul or a disciple who knew the mind of his teacher very well) was envisaging the baptism of believers. Nor need this be a partial view. There was a time in the history of New Testament exegesis, in the middle of the twentieth century, when it seemed that scholars of all church traditions had accepted the Baptist argument that there was no evidence in the New Testament for the baptism of infants, and that the earliest available witness for this practice was from the third century. It seemed there was widespread agreement that New Testament baptism, in the first generation of missionary enterprise, was conversion-baptism, linked with the confession of faith that 'Jesus is Lord'. There seemed no need to argue about the historic issues any longer, although these in themselves were not of course sufficient to refute a theological case for the development of infant baptism in the early Church of post-apostolic times. In recent years there has been a swing back to earlier views that traces of infant baptism can be found in the New Testament writings, placing more weight on – for example – the record that whole households were baptized. But a strong case can still be made that the *paradigm* for baptism in such passages as Ephesians 4 is that of the baptism of someone who has heard the word of the gospel, repented and believed in Christ.

The context for the celebration of the seven unities of the Christian Church in Ephesians 4.4-6, which are trinitarian in character, seems to be that of baptism. As commentators point out, the items have not been chosen haphazardly, but because they all relate in some way to the baptismal rite. In particular there are the three closely interconnected unities of 'one Lord, one faith, one baptism', which might be expanded as 'One Lord, the object of faith's confession in baptism'.[5] The 'one faith' is to be given a primarily objective meaning, as the substance of faith which is avowed by the one being baptized; but the objective cannot be separated from the subjective, as confession involves an attitude of trust. Faith and baptism are closely linked, since baptism is 'the supreme occasion of the confession of faith as it is faith's embodiment, subjectively and objectively'.[6] This reading is confirmed by a saying a little later in the same letter, that the Church as the bride of Christ has been 'cleansed by the washing of water with the word' (Ephesians 5.26). The meaning of 'word' should probably be given the widest range, including the proclamation of the gospel, the confession made by the candidate for baptism ('Jesus is Lord') and the baptismal formula of the triune name pronounced over the one baptized. Thus, as one Baptist New Testament scholar puts it, 'The baptism that sanctifies and cleanses is that in which the Word is heard, confessed and submitted to by the baptized.'[7]

Whether or not young children were baptized at this period, the context of the text about one baptism is that of conversion-baptism. It would be going beyond the evidence available in the New Testament to rule out the inclusion of young children, at least occasionally, in baptisms of whole households. We might say that the case is not proven. But it would be more extraordinary, given the lack of a single overt reference to the baptism of infants, to make infant baptism normative for the meaning of baptism. Among those who have, nevertheless, followed this track, have been Reformed theologians who have identified baptism as a replacement for circumcision as the sign of the new covenant. Rather, if one wants to understand the meaning of the baptism that unites all Christian people, then the model to be looked at is the baptism of someone who believes for himself or herself, for whom baptism is the meeting-place between a gracious God and a penitent human being.

All texts of Scripture have an afterlife, beyond the intention of the writers. The word of witness to Christ comes alive in new ages and new circumstances; the expansion of meaning which belongs to the living word does not contradict the original intention of the writers and the community to which they belonged, but it cannot be restricted to it. It does not follow, therefore, that the scope of one baptism must for us be limited to the baptism of believers. The question is one of perspective, a direction into which theological thinking is to be guided. When the Creed of Nicaea-Constantinople formulated the phrase 'one baptism for the forgiveness of sins', it was in a situation where there was already a widespread practice of the baptism of infants alongside the baptism of adult believers (as well as the challenging issue of how to deal with baptisms practised in communities condemned as heretical). The New Testament text was taking on new meaning to address the context, but we must be careful not to read this situation back into the New Testament text, as if the affirmation 'one baptism' simply validates 'common baptism' by identifying all practices of baptism as the same thing. In fact, the meaning of the phrase should be controlled, not only by the normative model of believers' baptism, but even more by the truly theological concept of the baptism experienced by Jesus Christ in his life, death and resurrection. There is one baptism because there is one Lord, who was immersed into the terrible desolation of sin and death for all humanity and raised from the waters of chaos by the power of the Spirit of God. As the report *Believing and Being Baptized* expresses it:

> transcending all our imperfect perceptions of baptism, our divisions, and whatever time gaps are involved in the process of Christian growth, there is still one immersion into the death and resurrection of Jesus through the Spirit. This we understand to be the intention of the scriptural text, 'one Lord, one faith, one baptism' (Ephesians 4.5). It is in accord with Jesus' portrayal of his crucifixion as a baptism, as immersion into the dark waters of death (Mark 10.38-39); this is the baptism in which we share in union with Christ. There is therefore, we believe, one baptism despite diversity of practice, and this need not be reduced to a notion of 'common baptism'.[8]

Returning to Ephesians 4.5 and 5.26, we notice that the author links the cleansing of the Church 'by the washing of water with the word' with the act of Christ in giving himself up for the Church (5.25), implying surely that the death of Christ is the primary baptism.

Now, if we take the redemptive act of Christ as our central image for 'one baptism', certain conclusions follow about the nature of baptism. In the first place, the act of baptism must be as unrepeatable as the drama of redemption, and this will be an aspect of the meaning of the phrase 'one baptism', whether or not it was explicitly in the mind of the author of Ephesians 4.5. Second, we see that – as in salvation itself – the grace of God displayed in baptism is always prevenient, 'going before' us, drawing us to God's self when we are still helpless and in the darkness of sin. This is the character of the covenant relationship which God establishes with created beings; as covenant-maker, God always takes the initiative, either to create the covenant in an eternal decree, or to remake it when it has been broken by unfaithfulness from the human side. It seems odd to Baptists, however, when it is argued that infant baptism is the supreme example of this grace of God that comes to human beings before it enters their hearts to come to God; sometimes it seems as if it is being urged that infant baptism follows naturally from the prevenient love of God in redemption itself.[9] While a very young infant is certainly unable to take the initiative in turning to God in faith and trust, this is because an infant cannot make *any* responsible decisions in life. How much more, we might say, is the prevenient grace of God exhibited when people who can make their own confession of faith and trust gladly acknowledge the wonder of Christ's self-giving that has preceded their own, and the overwhelming love of God that has enabled them to make their response in the first place. Baptists, as already remarked, will doubt whether the baptism of infants can express the whole range of the grace of God as fully as the baptism of believers. Infant baptism can certainly symbolize the prevenient grace of God, and the promise that lies within it, and has certain strengths in doing this; but to assert that it symbolizes prevenient grace *better* than believers' baptism is in effect to make the baptism of infants the normative model for baptism. This is where the perspective set up by the 'one baptism' of Ephesians 4 becomes important in the development of the doctrine of baptism. The same New Testament writings that present, overtly, the baptism of those who already believe, also emphasize the prevenient grace of God and find that the one reinforces the other. The priority of grace within the mysterious intersection between divine initiative and human response becomes evident precisely in the baptism of the believer.

A third conclusion we may draw from identifying the 'one baptism' as the death and resurrection of Jesus is that baptism is always a relational act. Christ is baptized, in water and in blood, in solidarity with the whole of humankind; his act, embedded in human relationships, transforms them for ever. Moreover, the representational aspect of atonement, in which Christ uniquely stands for humanity before God, leans upon the general truth that any human being can, to a limited extent, represent others and stand in their place. This should lead us to oppose any view of baptism as an individualistic act of private piety. The faith of the one baptized is supported by the faith of the whole Christian community, and in turn helps to renew the faith of the community which gathers around the baptismal pool. Any baptism is the occasion for the reaffirmation of the baptismal vows of all. As with prevenient grace, however, it is hard for Baptists to see how the baptism of infants is a *better* exemplification of this truth. Were this so, then infant baptism would again be the normative form. Since infants cannot make a confession of faith, there will certainly be a vicarious element in the faith of the parents, sponsors and congregation; they exercise faith when the infant cannot, praying for the activity of God in this young life until he or she can make his or her own response to God. Baptists think that the faith of the Church has a similar place in the service of presentation of infants. In the blessing of the child there is (at least) a proclamation of the gospel, prayer for the child which 'provides a channel for the grace of God to work'[10] in his or her life, and an acceptance of the child into the sphere of God's gracious influence in the community. The report *Believing and Being Baptized* puts it in this way:

> It can be said that the child's relationship to God is 'affected' through this blessing, not in any mechanical or magical way, but in so far as a new relationship is being made with the community of the Church in which God is at work through his grace. The love of God towards the child has not of course changed, as if it were not present before; the child is already within the orbit of the love of God through living in his world, but he or she needs to be positively accepted by the Church into the 'embrace of the Body' to deepen this influence.[11]

But there must be a limit to what human beings can do for each other in the dynamic of salvation; the faith of the Church cannot entirely replace the faith of the child. Only Christ can fully represent others before God, as the eternal mediator. Only in Christ is there a radical one-sidedness, in which the trust of Christ in the Father is 'reckoned as righteousness' for us, and has the power to create this trust within us. Human beings can, only to a certain degree, stand in each other's place as they each respond to the grace of God, and the baptism of a believer gives special opportunity for this mutuality, in the interplay between the faith of candidate and congregation.

A Baptist understanding of 'one baptism' is thus guided by the conviction that this baptism is nothing less than the drama of redemption acted out by Christ, and that his immersion into death and rising to new life is most fully expressed in the baptism of a believer. However, the affirmation of 'one baptism' brings a challenge to Baptists in the present situation of the Church universal, with its various baptismal practices. The writer of Ephesians 4 assumes in the phrase 'one baptism' that all Christians are bound together by their baptism, as they are by their one faith and one Lord. Whatever this meant in his day, we have to hear it in our time, when Baptists are apparently happy to recognize millions across the world as fellow-Christians regardless of their baptism. When Baptists reject infant baptism as no baptism at all, they dismiss too easily the hurt protest of those so baptized that they are unchurching them. They dispose of the charge with an emphatic (and perhaps amazed) denial that any such thought was in their minds. Baptists have gladly recognized infant-baptizing churches as true churches, while declining to recognize their practice of the sacrament of baptism, because they have appealed to the argument that it is faith that makes the Church, not baptism. Likewise, in their own congregational life, open membership churches in England (the majority of Baptist churches) admit those baptized only as infants, less because of a positive theological evaluation of infant baptism, than because a profession of personal faith has been considered to be the essential element for membership. There is a long Baptist history of recognizing that the risen Lord gives the blessing of his presence at the communion tables of infant-baptizing churches, while regarding their practice of baptism as being a failure in obedience to Christ.

Baptists, however, need to ask themselves whether the link between 'true baptism' and 'true church' can be dismissed so easily. From the seventeenth to the late nineteenth centuries, there were of course many Baptists who did insist strongly that entrance to the Church of Christ, according to the Scriptures, was through both faith and baptism. This was the almost universal view among General Baptists, and was also widespread among Particular Baptists. It was backed up not only by reference to Scripture, but by appeal to the Reformers' dictum that a true church is one where the word of God is rightly preached and the sacraments are rightly administered. This conviction was worked out in closed communion, or at least closed membership. The link between baptism and membership of the church was loosened by the desire to admit, first to the table and then to full membership, those who believed that they were truly baptized as infants. The assertion that it was faith alone, regardless of baptism, that constitutes the Church, was made for excellent motives: it was for the sake of preserving the unity of the body of Christ, of accepting those in whose lives the fruits of the Spirit of God could be clearly seen, and of respecting the Baptist principle of freedom of conscience. Frequent reference was made to Paul's appeal in Romans 15.7, 'Accept one another as Christ has accepted you'.[12] Those convinced of the truth of believers' baptism were not to judge those who disagreed with them; all must answer for their own convictions before the final judgement of their own master, Christ (Romans 14.3-5). While this approach was shaped by an Enlightenment concern for the 'sacred right of private judgement', it was thus also marked by a more scriptural view of eschatological judgement.

In the recent survey *Baptist Worship Today*, it became apparent that only 17 per cent of churches in the Baptist Union of Great Britain today require believers' baptism for people to be members in any way; 51 per cent admit to full membership on profession of faith alone, and another 24 per cent admit to a kind of associate membership without believers' baptism.[13] Open communion and membership has served Baptists well, in making possible their participation in ecumenical relations, and especially in enabling the sharing of congregational life and mission with Christian churches which practise infant baptism. It has been the necessary basis for Local Ecumenical Partnerships and especially single-congregation ventures. But the failure to develop a more thoroughgoing theology which could support such openness has led to difficulties today. While open membership congregations do not *require* those baptized as infants to be baptized again as believers, if this openness is based mainly on freedom of conscience before God then there is no theological reason for *refusing* 're-baptism' when it is asked for out of an instructed conscience. This has caused deep hurt among other churches with whom Baptists desire to work in partnership. Moreover, giving no recognition to infant baptism has had the result that those unbaptized in any mode may be admitted to membership, undermining the significance of baptism; this is a development certainly not intended by Baptist advocates of open membership in the past.

Baptists may have arrived at a point in their history when a theological assessment of infant baptism has become necessary. Is it possible to restore the close link between baptism and church membership, to keep a proper pastoral sensitivity towards the myriad of Christians who believe that they are truly baptized as infants, and also to preserve the Baptist conviction that the recovery of the apostolic practice of believers' baptism will foster the health of the Church? These are the questions to which the affirmation of 'one baptism' urges us.

common initiation

A way forward may lie in regarding baptism as one moment in a larger process of initiation, or the beginning of the Christian life. In the past Baptists have compared the events of one baptism with another; the question has been, 'Is infant baptism true Christian baptism?' But we need to set baptism in the context of salvation, which the New Testament presents less as a moment than as a journey of life, a 'pilgrim's progress'. Different writings give us three senses or tenses for salvation. Christians 'have been saved' through the once-for-all event of the cross of Jesus (e.g. Ephesians 2.8); we are 'being saved' as we are grow day by day in our healing relationship with God and are gradually made more like Christ (e.g. 1 Corinthians 1.18); we 'shall be saved' at the final appearing of Christ in glory (e.g. Romans 5.9-10). We cannot know the mysterious beginning of our salvation, far back in the secret purposes of God, who begins a work of prevenient grace in drawing human hearts to God's self. We cannot fully know what the end will be like, what it will really mean to have a body of glory and live a new creation. Whenever the process of salvation actually began for us, baptism can be a decisive point in the whole process of being saved. This is a meeting-place provided for us, to which God promises to come in order to meet our faith with divine grace, although we also meet God in many other times and places in life. While the whole of the Christian life is a saving process of growth into Christ, baptism is a moment within one stage of the journey of salvation, the early phase that we call 'beginnings' or initiation.

If baptism is truly to be a means of binding Christians together ('one baptism'), we must then compare not single moments – the baptism of an infant or a believer – but journeys, and this means listening to others' stories of their journey.[14] One journey, a Baptist experience, may be from infant blessing through Christian nurture in childhood to believers' baptism, laying on of hands for gifts of the Spirit, and then increasing use of those gifts in ministry in the world. An Anglican or Reformed journey might be from infant baptism, through Christian nurture in childhood, to public profession of faith, and laying-on of hands in confirmation for gifts of the Spirit, to be used in ministry in the world. Another journey that can be found in all churches would be from hearing the story of Jesus for the first time as an adult, repentance and conversion, believers' baptism, laying on of hands and consequent serving. This third kind of journey, familiar to all churches, underlines the fact that initiation is a process, since there has to be some kind of process between the moments of conversion and baptism. The first directing of conscious faith towards Christ will be initiated by the grace of God, and will be accompanied by an act of the Holy Spirit bringing the believer into fellowship with Christ. As James D. G. Dunn notes, in the thought of the Apostle Paul 'the Spirit is the beginning of the salvation process'; whatever relation this had in temporal sequence to water baptism, 'it was by receiving the Spirit that one became a Christian'.[15] If we want to affirm that believers are also 'incorporated into Christ' through water baptism, the 'beginning' of Christian life must be an extended process or journey and not a single point.

We are in a broken situation where churches have different beliefs about baptism, owing to different interpretations of Scripture and the different paths they have taken in history. Without abandoning their convictions, Baptists might be able to value and affirm someone's *whole* journey of experience, and not just the moment of public profession of faith on which attention is usually fixed; they might be able gladly to recognize how God has used every stage of the journey for saving purposes. Correspondingly, those who baptize infants as well as believers (since all churches practise believers' baptism in the case of older converts) might feel more free to offer some parents the option of delaying the baptism of their child until a later age, with the alternative of a service of infant blessing.

The often-quoted World Council of Churches report, *Baptism, Eucharist and Ministry*, did in fact propose that churches should seek mutually to recognize whole patterns of initiation. While its phrase 'common baptism' has become a touchstone for ecumenical discussion, the report was realistic in seeing that the mere fact that all churches practised some form of baptism would not in itself achieve the mutual recognition of each other's baptism as 'a sign and seal of our common discipleship'. It suggested that

> Churches are increasingly recognizing one another's baptism as the one baptism into Christ when Jesus Christ has been confessed as Lord by the candidate or, in the case of infant baptism, when confession has been made by the church (parents, guardians, godparents and congregation) *and affirmed later by personal faith and commitment.*[16]

The phrase 'and affirmed later' is clearly attached to the clause beginning 'when'. This is how, it suggests, mutual recognition is possible, when baptism is part of a whole journey into faith. What can be recognized by those practising believers' baptism, it suggests, is infant baptism plus a confession of personal faith. The commentary to clause 12 also spells out this mutual recognition of whole patterns or processes of initiation, stressing that both forms of baptism (infant and believers') need to be set in the context of Christian nurture, in which the baptized person – at any age – needs to grow in an understanding of faith:

> In some churches which unite both infant-baptist and believer-baptist traditions, it has been possible to regard as equivalent alternatives for entry into the church both a pattern whereby baptism in infancy is followed by a later profession of faith and a pattern whereby believers' baptism follows upon a presentation and blessing in infancy.

The article then urges all churches to consider whether they, too, cannot 'recognize equivalent alternatives in their reciprocal relationships'. That these equivalent alternatives are not simply the different forms of baptism but whole patterns of initiation is made clear by the 'clarification' of this clause offered by the official report on the responses made to *Baptism, Eucharist and Ministry*:

> Some churches ask what is meant by 'equivalent alternatives' . . . It is not the act of 'infant baptism' and the act of 'believers'/adult baptism' in themselves that are there proposed as 'equivalent alternatives', but rather two total processes of initiation which the text recognizes.[17]

That this had been intended all along was understood by the Baptist Union of Great Britain in its original response to *Baptism, Eucharist and Ministry*, when it commented that 'It has long been clear that a total process of Christian initiation wherein, at some point, all the necessary elements – including responsible faith-commitment – find a place offers the most promising way forward to mutual recognition on the baptismal issue.'[18] Other Baptist statements since then have underlined the desirability of comparing, not one isolated moment of baptism with another, but the whole sequence of events which marks the beginning of the Christian life and discipleship.[19] The Baptist view will be that the process of initiation has not come to an end until a baptismal candidate exercises his or her own faith in Christ. If this cannot be found within the event of baptism itself, as in the case of the baptism of infants, then initiation will have to be 'stretched' in some way to accommodate it. Traditionally this moment has been located in western churches within confirmation, but whether or not it takes this particular form, Baptists will expect personal faith (arising from divine grace) to be a part of Christian beginnings.

However, appeal to a common *process* of Christian beginnings, or to a common journey into faith and salvation, runs somewhat against the stream of another momentum of thought which has swelled larger since the publication of *Baptism, Eucharist and Ministry*. There is a widely held view among churches practising infant baptism that there should be a 'unified rite' of initiation, bringing the aspects which have been variously signified by baptism, chrismation/confirmation and first communion as close together as possible. The influence of the baptismal theology of the Orthodox Church here has been pervasive, but among western Protestant paedobaptist churches it has not led to a sequence of rites closely linked in time, but rather to a different kind of 'integration'. In this approach, the gift of the Spirit and incorporation into Christ is located entirely in the event of water baptism itself. Baptism is regarded as 'complete sacramental initiation'. Any act of anointing or laying on of hands that follows baptism, whether at the time (Orthodox chrismation) or later on (western confirmation) is not to be seen as part of sacramental initiation, though certainly to be understood as part of Christian growth.

Traditionally among western paedobaptist churches, there has been a kind of two-stage view of initiation or Christian beginnings. Despite the fact that confirmation was a late development in the West (ninth century), and despite ambiguity about whether candidates were confirming their faith or whether God was confirming (establishing) their salvation, some view of an extended process prevailed. The two rites might be understood as two sacramental acts in sequence, or two parts of the same sacrament divided in time.[20] In the Reformed tradition, completion of initiation in confirmation was thus seen to be necessary to leave place for the confession of personal faith. By contrast, however, the recent Toronto Statement on Christian initiation in the Anglican Communion, *Walk in Newness of Life* (1991), makes the unequivocal claim that 'Baptism is complete sacramental initiation and leads to participation in the Eucharist'.[21] The rite of confirmation is affirmed as having a continuing pastoral role as a means of renewal of faith among the baptized, or a reaffirmation of the baptismal covenant, but it is not to be seen in any way as a completion of initiation.[22]

This example shows the tensions that arise, however, with this approach. The authors of the report do not seem to be able to avoid entirely the image of a process of initiation, since they approve 'the recovery of the earlier tradition of the church that eucharist is in fact the fulfilment and sacramental completion of the initiatory process'.[23] This is despite the insistence elsewhere in the report that baptism alone is 'complete sacramental initiation'. If Eucharist is after all needed to complete the process, then why not confirmation or some similar occasion for a personal confession of faith? What perhaps is needed is a sacramental theology in which baptism, at whatever age, is not incomplete as baptism, but is incomplete as initiation.

A concept of common initiation will recognize that different baptismal practices share in some way in the 'one baptism' of Jesus Christ, without claiming that different modes of baptism are simply equivalent, or the same thing. It affirms that there is a process or journey of initiation in which baptism may stand either near the beginning (infant baptism) or near the end (believers' baptism), while Baptists will continue to urge that it is placed most appropriately and most meaningfully at the point where those baptized can exercise faith for themselves. This is the treasure that Baptists believe they have been allowed to guard for the Church universal. But for this picture of a journey to be convincing, and to move hearts and minds, we need constructively to develop a *theology* of initiatory process. This must support any attempt to compare 'equivalent processes', as *Baptism, Eucharist and Ministry* proposes. What we need is a theology, and not just a practice, of mutual acceptance. Here there are three dynamics which may help us, each being an interplay of balancing factors: there is the interplay between grace and faith, between Spirit and water, and between the Body of Christ and the Church.[24] All these depend on a theological view of baptism as immersion into the threefold fellowship of God who is Trinity. All of them are to be understood from the perspective given by believers' baptism, as a personal (but not private) encounter between God and human partners, rather than beginning from the viewpoint of infant baptism as – for instance – a sign of the covenant or an event of promise.

an interplay of grace and faith

Christian initiation as a process or journey is, first, characterized by an interplay of divine grace and human faith at all stages. The journey begins in the hidden depths of prevenient grace, at work beneath the surface of human life and consciousness, originating in the eternal desire of God for fellowship with human persons. We are called to respond to God's project in creation with trust and obedience, and initiation into this partnership for any person ends with his or her conscious and responsible response. At any stage in this process of making a partnership (or covenant), baptism can be a meeting-place between grace and faith and so can focus the two realities. We need to abandon the stereotypes that infant baptism only expresses divine grace, and that believers' baptism only witnesses to human faith.

However, we must recognize that the nature of grace and faith will be different at different stages of the journey, or at different phases of Christian nurture. Grace and faith are not blank counters. They indicate movements of relationship between God and human life – the self-giving movement of God towards creation and the trustful movement of human beings towards God. Grace and faith are aspects of participation in God, of being drawn into the interweaving movements of relationship in the triune life, which are like relations between a Father and Son, ever renewed and opened to the future by a life-giving Spirit. In the baptism or the blessing of an infant, the nature of faith is the corporate faith of the community and the vicarious faith of sponsors, full of hope for what this child can be. It is not the trusting response of the child himself or herself. The nature of grace is essentially prevenient, a surrounding of the child with the gracious presence of God, in and outside the church community, grace taking every opportunity to draw this child deeper into the life of God and God's mission in the world as he or she grows up. Faith will then show different characteristics at different stages of human development, sometimes defined as 'experienced', 'affiliative', 'searching' and 'mature' faith,[25] in a manner suitable for the stage in the journey; faith will be 'owned' by a person during the last two of these phases. In the baptism of a believer of responsible age or in some rite of commitment like confirmation, there will be the faith of the community and the owned faith of the individual. In turn this faith will be responding to grace which is not only prevenient but transformative, empowering the believer to share in God's own ministry of reconciliation. Since grace and faith are interwoven in relationship, the nature of God's gracious approach to a person is bound to differ according to the nature of human faith which is possible. For those who practise infant baptism and some later rite of renewal and commitment there are then not 'two stages' of initiation but a continuum with at least two focal points within it.

The statement of the influential Ely Report of the Church of England that after baptism 'there can be no place for further degrees of initiation' or 'no place for any degrees of being "in Christ" or "in the Spirit"'[26] therefore seems to reflect too static a view of the relation between God and human persons. There is, of course, an interplay between grace and faith throughout the whole of life as a baptismal process, a daily journey of dying and rising with Christ. But there is also a specific range of interplay that belongs to the period of initiation, extending over one section of the journey, a phase that we call the beginning. How then shall we demarcate the ending of this section, and say that initiation has come to an end? It cannot be a matter of salvation having been finished, since salvation must be a life-long (possibly an eternal) process of 'being saved', being transformed into the image of God which is visible in Christ. The section of the journey of salvation which is called initiation is surely best characterized as about becoming a disciple, about responding to the call to be a disciple and taking up the responsibilities of a disciple. Faith must become an ethical response before the beginning has come to an end. Thus far Karl Barth is right when he insists that the beginning of Christian life involves 'the grateful Yes of man to God's grace . . . [which] must become at once the Yes of a grateful work . . . to the foundation of the Christian life belongs the ready doing of this work'.[27] Though Barth adds immediately that this first step is 'empowered' by grace, he unfortunately divides the human 'Yes' from the divine 'Yes', baptism in water from baptism in Spirit, as two different moments. Baptists will agree with Barth that the 'grateful Yes' is most appropriately located in believers' baptism, but unlike Barth many will want also to locate God's 'Yes' in this event; Barth makes it purely a human act of obedience, responding to a prior baptism with the Holy Spirit.

Those who practise believers' or disciples' baptism will find it disclosing the particular kind of interplay of grace and faith that happens towards the end of the process; those practising infant baptism will have a focus on the particular interplay that happens near the beginning. Baptism, in this view, is always 'complete' for what it is: there is nothing defective about the presence of the kind of grace and faith appropriate to the point in the process where it happens. But in no case can baptism be complete initiation. In the case of infant baptism the later moment of freely accepted discipleship will also belong to the foundation or beginning of Christian life; Eucharist and confirmation (or some other rite of laying on hands) will not complete baptism, but they will complete initiation. In the case of believers' baptism, the apprehending of the person by God's grace before baptism, prior faith and first communion are all part of the process. Baptism in the triune Name is a sort of snapshot or freeze frame of a flowing movement, a moment symbolizing the whole but not containing the whole.

Baptists will naturally regret that the picture is taken so early with the baptism of infants; they will prefer that the particular interplay of grace and faith in the life of the young child be expressed in the rite of infant presentation and blessing. They think that in this action they follow the example of Jesus himself, who is recorded as taking children in his arms, laying hands on them and welcoming them into the community with a blessing (Mark 10.13-16; Matthew 19.13-15; cf. Matthew 18.3ff, Luke 18.15-17).[28] Baptists are surprised when these gospel passages are claimed to reflect a practice of infant baptism in the early church, since there is no obvious correspondence with the symbolism of water baptism. However, Baptist preference for infant blessing at an early stage of initiation does not mean that the act of infant baptism is to be regarded as simply equivalent to blessing, any more than that it is simply equivalent to believers' baptism; what should be compared are whole journeys of beginning. Baptism is freighted with a rich symbolism that is not applicable to infant blessing, and it shares in the 'one baptism' of Christ. If part of the Christian family uses the rite of baptism at an early stage of the journey, then this situation must be taken seriously. Baptists will think that an opportunity has been lost for the fullest expression of the symbolism of baptism; they will think that there is no 'easy fit' between the whole range of imagery that the New Testament applies to baptism, and the baptism of an infant. But that very symbolism will be undermined if it is used more than once. In particular, the unrepeatability of the 'one baptism' of Christ will no longer find expression.

Baptists have, for the most part, agreed that baptism is unrepeatable. Where they have baptized those who were previously baptized as infants, this is because they have not regarded infant baptism as 'baptism' at all. If it is understood as a kind of baptism which shares in any way in the 'one baptism' of Christ, even if it is not equivalent to believers' baptism, then it follows that someone should not be baptized in both modes. A Baptist will think that an opportunity has been sadly lost for focusing the grace of God and the faith of the believer, but it will also be lost, at times, in the practice of believers' baptism. Some may be baptized in their early teens, and come later to such a renewal of faith that they now find much more meaning in the act than they did at the time, and they wish to be baptized again. Baptist churches have usually refused to re-baptize such enquirers, and have instead encouraged them to look on their baptism as a moment when God met them in faithfulness and in fulfilment of the divine promise, however they felt, and that this very moment of meeting was the beginning of a process that has now come to a fullness of trust.

an interplay of Spirit and water

There has been a long dispute in the history of the Church about the relation of the Spirit to water baptism. Especially relevant to our concerns is the Pauline concept of the 'seal of the Spirit',[29] which has been a storm centre of different interpretations. The majority of New Testament scholars locate the 'seal' in water baptism as the primary endowment of the Spirit, enabling and accompanying the participation of the believer in the death and resurrection of Jesus, and giving the believer a foretaste of the reality of the new creation. It is thus a parallel concept to 'baptism in the Spirit' and coincides with baptism in water. Others detach the 'seal' from water baptism, placing it either before or afterwards. James Dunn argues, like Karl Barth, that the action of being 'stamped' (sealed) with the Spirit or 'immersed' (baptized) in the

Spirit is the gift of God which begins the process of salvation, and is separate in New Testament thinking from water baptism. He is concerned that the Church has given water baptism the prominence that is really due to the Spirit.[30] By contrast, Orthodox exegesis has followed the practice of the third-century church and located the 'seal' in an immediate post-baptismal rite of anointing, first recorded in the account of baptism by Hippolytus.[31] In this 'sacrament of the Holy Spirit' there is a 'personal coming of the Holy Spirit' as a 'gift' to the one baptized.[32] We should also observe that Pentecostalism has placed baptism in the Spirit after water baptism as a second blessing, and that this has been followed in a more flexible way by the modern charismatic movement. We might wonder whether this is a parallel development, or an after-echo, of the tradition of a post-baptismal anointing.

From this tradition of interpretation we might draw two conclusions. First, on the basis of New Testament exegesis, it is certainly proper to keep the metaphors of sealing and baptism as a means of expressing the activity of God's Spirit within water baptism. But second, the diversity of experience of the Church through the years shows that the activity of the Spirit cannot be confined within the moment of baptism. The Pauline writings witness to many operations, promptings and fillings of the Spirit in Christian experience; Aquinas speaks of many 'sendings' of the Spirit;[33] Karl Barth remarks that the Spirit makes 'many new beginnings'.[34] This should make us cautious about appealing to the seal of the Spirit to support a notion of completed initiation in baptism. We may say that there are different comings of the Spirit appropriate to various stages of the process of initiation, as well as to the whole life-long journey of Christian growth. Just as baptism provides a focus for grace and faith, so it also offers a focus for the coming of the Spirit; however, the Spirit actually comes to persons before and after the rite, at whatever age it is performed. The process of Christian growth is that of being drawn more deeply into the triune life of God, and the metaphor of 'coming' is one way of pointing to this increasing participation.

Baptists will think that the metaphor of 'sealing' makes full sense in the context of believers' baptism; but just as grace and faith have a particular nature within the two kinds of baptism, we might say the same of 'sealing with the Spirit'. With infant baptism it is bound to have more of a sense of a stamp of ownership and foretaste, while with believers' baptism it will be more strongly associated with the giving of spiritual gifts (*charismata*) for ministry in the Church and world. It is difficult to conceive of infants receiving *charismata*, since according to the New Testament presentation these are not gifts in the sense of permanent possessions, but dynamic acts of the Spirit here and now through a believer. As James Dunn puts it:

> Charisma is always an event, the gracious activity of God through a man [*sic*]. It is the actual healing, the miracle itself . . . it is the particular act of service as it is performed . . . the exercise of a spiritual gift is itself the charisma.[35]

This in itself is an argument for the extension of the period of initiation to the point when the Spirit can manifest *charismata* in human persons and commission them for responsible service in the world. Whether this is a laying on of hands within the occasion of the baptism of a believer, or in a rite many years after infant baptism, it is still part of beginnings. Just as in baptism the Spirit takes an element in the natural world – water – and uses it as a place of encounter with God for renewal of life, so the Spirit takes natural human faculties and opens them up as a place to manifest spiritual gifts. When this begins to happen it is the end of the beginning, the end of laying foundations. A woman or man has become a disciple.

an interplay of Christ's body and Church

In the New Testament writings, the phrase 'body of Christ' has three meanings – the risen and glorious body of Jesus who was crucified, the community of the Church, and the eucharistic bread in which the community shares.[36] While some scholars make a total identity between at least the first two senses,[37] and others separate them out,[38] we should probably regard these realities as interweaving, overlapping and conditioning each other rather than being simply the same thing. In this overlap there is room for process and development in Christian nurture.

To speak of a process of incorporation does not mean that someone moves from partial membership – as a young child, or new convert – to full membership as a believer come of age; this view has rightly been rejected in recent thought among infant-baptizing churches, on the grounds that one is either a member or not. Rather, we might envisage that, at different stages of the journey of initiation, a person may be related to each of the senses of 'the body of Christ' in a way appropriate to that stage. This is only possible to conceive because Christian nurture is about being drawn more deeply into the interweaving movements of the triune life. We are concerned with organic relationships in a community, with a belonging which takes diverse forms. Incorporation should then be conceived of as a journey or process of entering more deeply into the reality of the body, just as we have been thinking of grace, faith and the gifting of the Spirit.

This kind of journey may be of help with resolving puzzles about membership of the Body of Christ which are confronted by both Anglican and Baptist communions. For both, Baptists will think, there are problems in making an exact and exclusive match between membership and baptism. For Anglicans, the question surely arises as to whether the millions baptized as infants, who now have no living relationship with the Christian community, are nevertheless members of the body. For Baptists, there is the issue of believing children within the Church: they have not yet been baptized, but can it be denied that they are members of the body of Christ?

If we consider the second sense of the body of Christ – the Church – Baptists hesitate to apply the term 'member' to very young infants before they have exercised any faith for themselves. This is because they use the term in Paul's sense (1 Corinthians 12.12-13), in which being a member means being a limb of the whole organism of the Church, making its own active contribution to the way that Christ becomes material, tangible and visible in the world. This kind of membership can only be declared as a promise for the young child, to be fulfilled in due time. Baptists might, however, consent to the pronouncement by others that infants who are baptized become members of the body understanding it to mean that they are thereby welcomed and embraced by the Church, wrapped around by the body, and immersed into its prayers and ongoing pastoral care. Until a young child exercises his or her own trust in Christ, Baptists will regard this as 'membership' in the general sense of belonging within the community which is called 'the body of Christ'. Some who are baptized will not (at least in their lifetime) progress beyond this initial kind of membership, because they have not travelled on the journey of faith.

With regard to the first sense of the body of Christ – the person of Christ incarnate and glorified – relating to the body means belonging to the risen Christ who has continuity of identity with Jesus of Nazareth. It means being conformed to the movement of relationship in God which is like a Son relating to a Father, characterized by a self-giving (dying) and a newness of life (resurrection). By their human existence all persons participate in some way in God, in whom 'they live and move and have their being'; God makes room for the world in the fellowship of the divine life, and 'all things hold together' in Christ.[39] Through welcome into the Church which makes the dying and rising of Christ visible in the world, the infant will be drawn more deeply into the life of God, and so be shaped by the body of Christ in the first sense as well as the second. There is, then, a kind of incorporation which belongs to the stage of infancy – though Baptists will want to mark this by the blessing of an infant rather than by baptism.

At the end of the process of initiation – whether it has begun in infancy or in later life – a person relates to the body of Christ as a disciple, commissioned for service. The disciple is in covenanted relation with other disciples in the community of the Church, and exercises the spiritual gifts that characterize being a distinct limb or member of Christ, conformed to the person of Christ through an owned faith. This is not a full membership as contrasted with an earlier partial membership; it is the kind of membership appropriate to being a disciple of Christ on active service in the world, sharing in the mission of God. Between the beginning and the end of the phase of initiation, membership may be manifested in a variety of ways. A growing child, for instance, exercising a trust in Christ which is appropriate to being a child, will be an essential part of making the body of Christ visible. He or she is not yet commissioned as a disciple to work in the world (by believers' baptism or some kind of confirmation), but is still a member of the body, contributing a feature to the face of Christ which stands out in the community. A Baptist will want to affirm this as being true whether or not the child has been baptized in infancy.

At first sight it may seem that the words of the Apostle Paul in 1 Corinthians 12.12-14 stand against the naming of not-as-yet-baptized, but believing, children as members of the body of Christ:

> For just as the body is one and has many members, and all
> the members of the body, though many, are one body, so it is
> with Christ. For in the one Spirit we were all baptized into one
> body . . . Indeed, the body does not consist of one member but
> of many.

The point of the passage, however, is not to define who are, and
who are not, members of the body of Christ. Paul's aim is to
describe the unity of the body. As one commentator puts it,
'Indeed, despite the considerable literature on this text suggesting
otherwise, Paul's present concern is not to delineate how an
individual becomes a believer, but to explain how they, though
many, are one body'.[40] What makes them one in their diversity
is the reception of the one Spirit. Paul, then, is writing to those
who have been baptized, to urge them to use the gifts they have
been given by the Spirit on that occasion for the sake of the one
body of which they are individually members, and to value the gifts
of others. But we need not deduce from this text that those who
are on the way to baptism in water, and so as yet unbaptized, are
not already members of Christ through the Spirit, nor that they
have no contribution to make to the body. When they are baptized
as believers, they will of course be immersed more deeply into
the body.

equivalent stories

To accept a pattern of initiation which includes infant baptism, and
to acknowledge that this baptism shares in the 'one baptism' of
Christ, will obviously be a sharp challenge for Baptists. It will mean
recognizing that the journey of Christian beginnings has been
completed by someone who, having been baptized as an infant,
has grown in Christ to the point where he or she has made a
confession of faith and been commissioned for Christian service
(whether in confirmation or some other act). It will mean that
where people present themselves for membership in a Baptist
church, having only made part of this journey, the church will
enable them to complete it; they will not be offered another
baptism, but the opportunity to make profession of their faith
and to receive the commission of discipleship, and spiritual gifts
to fulfil it, through the laying on of hands.

A Baptist who accepts the argument in this paper is not being asked to regard infant baptism and the baptism of a believer as equivalent acts. As George Beasley-Murray, former Principal of Spurgeon's College, London, and the most accomplished Baptist New Testament scholar of the twentieth century, conceded towards the end of his life: 'while [baptism's] scriptural norm and most powerful expression is exhibited in the baptism of believers, room can be found for infant baptism as a valid accommodation of the norm'.[41] Baptism, he suggested, could be accommodated or adapted to infants if it were seen as essentially 'attesting the commencement of the work of grace within the baptized with a view to its blossoming into fullness of life in Christ and his Body the Church as the individual's life progressively opens to Christ'.[42] He proposed that infant baptism could be understood as giving powerful expression to one dimension within baptism – that of the prevenient grace of God. The present paper has actually found somewhat more continuity than this between the baptism of infants and believers, but it has also highlighted what Baptists firmly believe to be the differences, which make them uncomfortable with the notion of 'common baptism'. In the light of this, Beasley-Murray makes a further important observation. Those practising infant baptism might *themselves* apply the range of baptismal symbolism to the baptism of an infant in exactly the same way as in the baptism of a believer. In the language of this paper, we can say that they might themselves affirm an equivalence between the baptismal events, and so a common baptism, where a Baptist would not. But this should not lead Baptists, urges Beasley-Murray, to 'the dismissal of the rite [of infant baptism] itself'. There is a matter here of freedom of conscience and liberty of interpretation. He thus wrote:

> I make the plea that churches which practise believers' baptism should consider acknowledging the legitimacy of infant baptism, and allow members in Paedobaptist churches *the right to interpret it according to their consciences*. This would carry with it the practical consequence of believer-baptist churches refraining from baptizing on confession of faith those who have been baptized in infancy.[43]

But if the recognition of equivalent stories of initiation is to be the way forward for fuller fellowship between Baptist and Anglican churches, then there are also challenges to those practising infant baptism. First, they will have to ensure that they *do* provide for a significant moment of personal confession of faith, and public witness to that faith, during the process of nurture of the Christian disciple. This will mean giving higher profile to the moment of confirmation, or something like it, against the trend to downplay confirmation in favour of a single 'unified rite of initiation'. The recent Anglican–Methodist covenant in Great Britain gives some sign that this can happen, as the report states that 'In our churches baptism is generally seen as the essential first stage of a process of Christian initiation that includes Confirmation and participation in Communion', and 'Confirmation is regarded by both Churches as a means of grace within the total process of initiation.'[44]

Second, those practising infant baptism will have to take care that the child is indeed enabled to set out on the journey into faith. Baptism should only be offered where it is clear that the child will be part of the Christian community, surrounded by companions for the journey and committed to receiving Christian teaching, in an environment where the promises made in the baptism will have the opportunity to be fulfilled. Otherwise, Baptists hope that the open welcome of the church will be offered to parents through a service of infant blessing. While Baptists understand that Anglicans feel pain when faced by a situation in which 'second' baptisms happen, there is also pain for Baptists who have received baptism as an infant, who have grown up without any meaningful connection with the church or hearing of the Gospel of Christ, and who are then asked to forgo the baptism as a believer which they desire.

Let us be clear about the large step it will be for local Baptist churches to be persuaded (not coerced) to decline baptism to those already baptized as infants, against the definite request and 'instructed conscience' of the person concerned, who wants to be baptized as part of his or her growth in discipleship. If such enquirers are to be encouraged to find the gracious activity of God in their baptism as infants, and to complete their initiation (if they have not already done so) by laying on of hands instead of a new baptism, then churches must be able to see that there are two alternative paths for Christian beginnings which are truly comparable. The journeys, though placing baptism at different points, must equally offer opportunities for God's grace, human faith and human obedience to Christ to be displayed. This makes a third challenge for Anglicans, as Baptists see things. It means that churches baptizing infants must be seen to be respecting the integrity of those who follow both kinds of journey, and thus treating sympathetically those parents in their fellowship who want their newborn children to receive a blessing rather than baptism. Parents who prefer that their children should wait to be baptized until a later time of personally-owned faith should not be made to feel that they have ill-founded scruples, or are depriving their children of the advantages of belonging within the Church.

The way forward in partnership between Anglicans and Baptists, avoiding the hurt that has been caused by baptismal practices on both sides, cannot be that of a simplistic 'common baptism'. The situation is too complicated and fraught with the memories of past pain for that. But the way forward can be through a sensitive recognition of sharing in 'one baptism' through different stories of initiation. Then it can be truly said, with a flash of recognition: 'It's the same story!'

chapter five

one baptism:
an Anglican contribution

Both the Bible and the Creed speak of 'one baptism'. It is a
scriptural expression as well as a credal one. That is a rather
overwhelming combination: there could hardly be greater
authority for the Church than Scripture and the Creed of
Nicaea-Constantinople! Clearly there is something of enormous
significance in the phrase 'one baptism', that both the Bible and
the Creed should use it. But what does the phrase signify? Taken
on its own, 'one baptism' can be merely an ecumenical slogan.
But if we probe beneath the surface of this expression we find a
theological truth that is important to all churches that baptize,
even though their theology and practice of baptism may not be
in complete harmony. This is true, for example, of Anglicans
and Baptists.

the biblical basis of one baptism

It is in the context of an appeal for unity in the Spirit that
Ephesians 4.4-6 states: 'For there is one body and one Spirit, just
as you were called to the one hope of your calling, one Lord, one
faith, one baptism [*hen baptisma*], one God and Father of all, who
is above all and through all and in all.' Here we have what Andrew
Lincoln in his commentary calls 'a series of seven acclamations of
oneness'. They recount the 'unifying realities' of the faith, on which
the appeal for unity in the Spirit is based. They comprise what
Lincoln dubs the 'foundational unities', the 'distinctive realities' of
the Christian life. The order in which they are given is thought by
Lincoln to be dictated by compositional or rhetorical considerations,
rather than by the logic of experience, though there is perhaps
something to be said on the other side.

The passage, especially verse 5, is thought to echo earlier credal
or confessional material and probably has a baptismal context.
The expression 'one faith' is to be taken in the objective sense,
referring to the content of what is believed (as in 4.13 and
Colossians 1.23 and 2.7), rather than in the subjective sense

of the faith that believes, though of course the two are interrelated. The overall thrust of this text is that the Church's unity is grounded in the unity of God and reflects that divine unity. Lincoln points the moral for the ecumenical quest: 'When the church fails to maintain and express unity, it radically undermines the credibility of its belief in the one God.'[1]

Although these seven affirmations refer to the massive 'givens' of the Christian faith, the list in Ephesians is not exhaustive. It is often noted that the Eucharist or Lord's Supper is not included; neither is there any mention of the ministry, especially that of pastoral oversight. The likely baptismal setting may suggest that the themes mentioned here belong to the beginning of the process of Christian initiation: calling, faith in Christ, baptism into the one body by the one Spirit. It was perhaps not part of the author's purpose to carry the story forward to the completion of the process of initiation in sacramental communion with Christ and his Body in the Eucharist. By the same token, the passage does not mention confirmation or the laying on of hands. The role of formal confirmation at the time of this epistle is uncertain – though baptism and the laying on of hands are linked in Acts (8.14-17; 9.17-18; 19.5-6); in Hebrews (6.2); and may be implied in the Pastorals (cf. 1 Timothy 6.12 and 2 Timothy 1.6; cf. Titus 3.5-6).

The expression 'one baptism' in Ephesians remains tantalizingly cryptic. We should not try to read too much into it. Calvin warns against inferring directly from the text that baptism is unrepeatable, though of course he believes that it is. The point that the Apostle (as Calvin calls him) is making is simply that one baptism is common to and unites all Christians.[2] That in itself is a major affirmation with huge ecumenical implications. It is this mystery of the common baptism, the one and undivided baptism that we hope to explore here. We begin with Anglican testimony from Richard Hooker and Thomas Cranmer (the Thirty-nine Articles and the service for the public baptism of infants in *The Book of Common Prayer*, 1662 – both of which remain doctrinal standards for the Church of England).

Anglican aspects of 'one baptism'

Richard Hooker cites Ephesians 4.4-6 as his key text when he defines the nature of the visible Church of Christ. For Hooker the formula sums up the revealed, God-given 'essence' of Christianity.

It comprises what all its members have in common: 'that *one Lord* whose servants they all profess themselves, that *one Faith* which they all acknowledge, that *one Baptism* wherewith they are all initiated'. Hooker implies that the one Lord, the one faith and the one baptism hold together the visible and the mystical dimensions of the Church, the external profession and the spiritual reality: 'The visible Church of Jesus Christ is therefore one, in outward profession of those things, which supernaturally appertain to the very essence of Christianity, and are necessarily required in every particular Christian man.'[3]

Unlike Calvin, Hooker deduces the impossibility of second baptism precisely from this text. He does not pull any punches on this point: 'Iteration of baptism once given hath been always thought a manifest contempt of that ancient apostolic aphorism, "One Lord, one Faith, one Baptism".' Hooker adds that baptism is 'one' not only in the sense that it offers the same grace to all persons, but also because 'it ought not to be received by any one man above once'. It represents a once-for-all event, the union of the Christian with the death and resurrection of Christ. Baptism can no more be repeated than a person can be born naturally more than once, or than Christ can die and rise again more than once. 'Second baptism was ever abhorred in the Church of God as a kind of incestuous birth.'[4]

Cranmer's Thirty-nine Articles do not explicitly comment on 're-baptism', but it is significant that *The Book of Common Prayer* service for the public baptism of infants begins with the question, 'Hath this child been already baptized or no?' Only if the answer is in the negative will the service proceed. (*On the Way* insists that 'the once for all character of baptism reflects the once for all given-ness of Jesus Christ (Ephesians 4.4-6) and cannot be treated as negotiable in the initiation practice of the Church of England'.)[5]

Underlying Hooker's vehemence on the issue of 're-baptism' is his profound sense of the living union, constituted sacramentally through the action of the Holy Spirit, between Christ and his Church. They are one flesh as well as one spirit. Hooker's language is that of mutual indwelling, of nuptial union and of 'mystical conjunction'. His metaphors are organic and physical. 'The Church is in Christ as Eve was in Adam . . . God made Eve of the rib of Adam. And his Church he frameth out of the very flesh, the very wounded and bleeding side of the Son of Man.' He seems to be saying that the true Sacrament (he uses the word 'elements') behind the sacraments is 'his body crucified and his blood shed for the life of the world'.[6] There is a hint of the modern idea of Jesus Christ as the great primal sacrament of salvation.

Hooker's sacramental language is close to Cranmer's in *The Book of Common Prayer*, especially to the Prayer of Humble Access, which itself echoes John 6 and 15 ('Grant us, therefore, gracious Lord, so to eat the flesh of thy dear Son Jesus Christ, and to drink his blood, that our sinful bodies may be made clean by his body, and our souls washed through his most precious blood, and that we may evermore dwell in him and he in us'). It also speaks the same language as the second post-communion prayer ('thou . . . dost assure us thereby that we are very members incorporate in thy mystical body' (1552)).

Hooker's is a realist sacramental theology. The sacraments do not simply teach Christian truth; they are not mere memorials or acts of witness. They are instrumental means of grace: 'they really give what they promise and are what they signify'. Just as we receive the sacraments on or in our bodies, so we receive the grace they signify. In both baptism and the Eucharist we receive Christ.[7]

Once again, Hooker is very close to the Church of England's formularies. Article XXV states: 'Sacraments ordained of Christ be not only badges or tokens of Christian men's profession, but rather they be certain sure witnesses, and effectual signs of grace, and God's good will towards us, by the which he doth work invisibly in us, and doth not only quicken, but also strengthen and confirm our Faith in him.' Article XXVII develops the point:

> Baptism is not only a sign of profession, and mark of difference, whereby Christian men are discerned from others that be not christened, but it is also a sign of Regeneration or new Birth, whereby, as by an instrument, they that receive Baptism rightly are grafted into the Church; the promises of the forgiveness of sin, and of our adoption to be the sons of God by the Holy Ghost, are visibly signed and sealed; Faith is confirmed, and Grace increased by virtue of prayer unto God.

Although in Hooker the emphasis is on divine action, rather than on human reception and response, the latter are clearly affirmed. The sacraments do not act physically upon us, Hooker points out, but are 'moral instruments' requiring our 'duties of service and worship' (probably a deliberate echo of the post-communion prayer in *The Book of Common Prayer* (1559), which itself echoes Romans 12.1). Without these they remain unprofitable. The sacraments are not absolutely necessary to salvation, but they are the divinely appointed normal means by which saving grace is conveyed and our part is to be obedient to the revealed will of God.[8]

Article XXV also stresses that the sacraments do not work automatically, but require appropriate human receptivity: 'And in such only as worthily receive the same they have a wholesome effect or operation: but they that receive them unworthily purchase to themselves damnation, as Saint Paul saith.'

The central idea in Hooker and in the Thirty-nine Articles is of baptism as an 'effectual sign', but one that functions only in the context of prayer, faith and the life of the Christian community. This is a paradox that needs further exploration. There is a tensive logic in the position that affirms both the initiative of grace and the indispensability of human response; that speaks of a God-given effectual sign, but stresses that its effectiveness depends on prayer and faith; that has a high biblical view of baptism as union with Christ in his death and resurrection, and then blithely applies that to the baptism of those who are not yet old enough to answer for themselves. What holds this tension together? What gives integrity to this classical Anglican approach?

The key to understanding this paradox is that this baptismal theology is articulated within a particular tradition of epistemology or philosophy of knowledge. It is a tradition that has been decisively shaped by Scripture and by patristic theology in its Platonic mode, not least as that is found in St Augustine of Hippo. The approach is relational, personalist and dynamic. In these Anglican Reformation sources the gift of grace in baptism is not reified. It is not a something injected into a person that magically changes the substance of a person. It is a covenantal transaction whereby a person is initiated into the Body of Christ – the mystical community that is the special sphere of Christ's presence and of the activity of the Holy Spirit – and thereby acquires the privileges and obligations of that community. Only the language of covenant, relationship, process, divine promise and human response, and communion is adequate to describe the event of baptism. As the previous paper, written from a Baptist perspective, has already argued, baptism is the focal sacramental event in a process of Christian initiation. Though baptism is the pivotal event of this process, other elements are also vital. As an unfolding process by which the grace of God is received and appropriated, Christian initiation is necessarily extended in time, even if certain crucial moments are sometimes compressed together. It constitutes a journey into Christ and his Church. The initiation is not complete until the journey has been completed and the process has run its full course. It includes instruction in the faith, personal profession of faith, strengthening for service by the Holy Spirit and admission to Holy Communion. The package should be seen as a whole.

The elements that, from a human point of view, make this process fruitful and effective for those who are baptized are faith, prayer and obedience, all qualities that belong to discipleship. But this discipleship is conceived corporately, not individualistically. There is a strong sense of vicariousness, of 'on behalf of'. Christ does for us what we cannot do for ourselves and we as Christians do for our fellows what they cannot yet do for themselves in order that they may eventually perform it. The aspect of 'on behalf of' is perhaps most pronounced when a young child is brought for baptism. The faith, prayer and commitment are those of the parents, the godparents and the congregation as together they hold the child before God.

Cranmer's baptism service (as Stephen Sykes has pointed out[9]) takes the form of a covenant between God and the child, initiated from God's side. There are three key elements in this.

First, the theme of promising: Sykes describes the promises made by the godparents in the name of the child as constituting a hinge in the service on which the grace of baptism turns. They are simply the human response to God's promises declared in the gospel, particularly the promise to answer prayer. There is what Sykes calls a 'positive battery of references to promise', both God's and ours.

Second, the stress on receiving: the word 'receive' occurs ten times in the baptismal liturgy. We receive God's grace in the sacrament. Christ receives us into his Church.

Third, the example of Christ taking the children in his arms, which includes both promise and reception: Sykes describes 'the emotionally powerful image of the child being embraced in the arms of Jesus' mercy' as 'the affective heart of this liturgy'. He argues that Cranmer's liturgy 'was, by reason of its structure, drama and repetitions, a liturgy proclaiming Christ's reception of little children. When the priest at the height of the drama takes the child into his arms he is doing what Christ himself did. The congregation witnesses Christ's own embrace.'

The relational element is further affirmed when the priest, holding the child in his arms, says: 'We receive this Child into the congregation of Christ's flock', and the theme of discipleship is reinforced when the priest immediately goes on to say, 'and do sign *him* with the sign of the Cross, in token that hereafter *he* shall not be ashamed to confess the faith of Christ crucified, and manfully to fight under his banner, against sin, the world and the devil: and to continue Christ's faithful soldier and servant unto *his* life's end.' There can be little doubt that Article XXVII has in mind the gospel passage of Jesus taking the children in his arms (Matthew 19.13-15; cf. 18.1-14) when it affirms: 'The Baptism of young Children is in any wise to be retained in the Church, as most agreeable with the institution of Christ.'

Perhaps the most impressive Anglican advocate of a relational, personalist and social theology of baptism is Frederick Denison Maurice (1805–72). Baptism is one of six 'signs of a spiritual society', the Kingdom of Christ. It witnesses to what God has already done in Christ. Baptism is not a human work, nor is its grace a human property or possession. The grace of baptism is covenantal, bringing the Christian into the life-giving milieu in which Christ is encountered, confessed and obeyed. In baptism we claim our birthright, our position in Christ. Maurice had an insight into Martin Luther's theology, rare among nineteenth-century Anglicans. He makes Luther say: 'Believe on the warrant of your baptism. You are grafted into Christ; claim your position.' Baptism proclaims for every Christian that they are 'taken into union with a divine Person'. But this truth rests upon another: 'that there is a society for mankind which is constituted and held together in that Person'. Beyond that truth lies the unity of the triune God. For Maurice, our primary Christian duty is to have faith in, to actualize, the baptismal union between Christ, the Christian and the Church. Maurice's heightened relational language reaches its peak when he says that baptism initiates us into 'an eternal and indissoluble friendship' with Christ.[10]

baptism and Christology

The expression 'one baptism' signals that baptism cannot be divided. There is, in a real sense, one great baptism, in which we all participate. There are not innumerable discrete acts of baptism, performed by some individuals and received by others. Even the expression common among Christians, 'my baptism', can be misleading. Nor are there baptisms belonging to various Christian churches in contradistinction from the baptisms of other churches: Anglican baptism, Lutheran baptism, Roman Catholic baptism, or even Baptist baptism.

There is one baptism because there is one Lord Jesus Christ – the unique, indivisible Saviour. There is one baptism because there is one, unique, unrepeatable saving action of God in the death and resurrection of God's only Son. The sacramental action of baptism represents and sets forth the dying and rising again to new life of Jesus Christ and our dying and rising in union with him – our justification, sanctification and glorification. It is the seismic effect of the baptism of Jesus, culminating in his death and resurrection, that makes Christian baptism the sacrament of justification, enabling St Paul to say, with a clear allusion to baptism: 'You were washed, you were sanctified, you were justified in the name of the Lord Jesus and in the Spirit of our God' (1 Corinthians 6.11).

In his own baptism, Jesus consecrated himself to his divine calling and God-given destiny. He also pioneered the way for his disciples by undergoing baptism as a representative person. His baptism at the hands of John the Baptist makes sense only if it was motivated by a sense of vocation that he already felt, if he took this step as part of God's path for him that he had already embraced. Jesus' reply to John's challenge to the propriety of what he was asking for, 'thus it is fitting for us to fulfil all righteousness' (Revised Standard Version), seems to be an echo of Isaiah 53.11: 'By his knowledge shall the righteous one, my servant, make many to be accounted righteous'.[11] The Suffering Servant of Deutero-Isaiah is a representative, corporate persona (just as is the Son of Man in Daniel 7.14). Messiahship itself – anointing to effect deliverance for the people – is representative.[12] By this act of solidarity with Israel at the River Jordan, Jesus is proleptically numbered with the transgressors, begins to bear the sins of many and to make intercession for them (Isaiah 53.12).

So Jesus' baptism was an act of obedience and of surrender to the Father's will. By it he charted the course that would lead him to Calvary and beyond. He looked back to what happened at the Jordan as the source of his authority. His teasing refusal to set out his credentials so that the Pharisees could impugn them probably contains an allusion to that event (Mark 11.30).[13]

As the shape of Jesus' destiny became clearer, the meaning of his baptism loomed larger in his consciousness. He saw its symbolism of descent and ascent as the prophetic enactment of his humiliation and subsequent vindication, suffering and deliverance, death and resurrection.

As he approached Jerusalem, Jesus hinted darkly at the 'baptism that he was to be baptized with' (Luke 12.49f.; cf. Mark 10.38f.). A study of the imagery of fire and water in the Hebrew Bible shows that here Jesus connected metaphorically what happened at the Jordan with the baptism of the fire of judgement that he would undergo for the salvation of the world and the mighty waters of affliction that would cover him in death. The baptismal imagery indicates that his physical baptism also prefigured the bursting from the tomb, the rising to God in glory and the waters of new life that would flow, as it were, from his side for the healing of the nations.[14]

The true, real baptism is, therefore, the great divine-human drama of redemption, from incarnation to glorification and the outpouring of the Holy Spirit – the drama of redemption in which God incorporated our humanity into his own divine life. The sacramental act of baptism is the powerful effective symbol of our incorporation into that total event. 'Christ's vicarious baptism was his whole living passion culminating in his death, his baptism in blood, once and for all accomplished on the cross' (T. F. Torrance). 'The baptism of Jesus is his whole existence in the form of a servant' (J. Robinson).[15]

He died and rose for us; we died and rose in him. This unity between Christ and the Christian is grounded in God's election of those who are to be saved. It is effected through the prevenient inward work of the Holy Spirit. It is received by faith. It is entered into sacramentally through baptism. It is set forth, strengthened and renewed in the Eucharist. It is appropriated in the ongoing life of fellowship and discipleship.

Because baptism is so intimately bound up with the person and work of Christ, it partakes of the once for all given-ness of his finished work. Baptism speaks primarily of something given already by God, a wonderful reality, into which we can be brought. As Cullmann suggests, the great act of baptism was carried out on Calvary entirely without our cooperation as sinners (though not, of course, without human involvement through the representative, perfect humanity of Jesus Christ). Through the cross and resurrection the whole world was baptized on the ground of the sovereign act of God, who in Christ 'first loved us' (1 John 4.19).[16]

Of course, baptism also involves a vital element of human response. There is a gospel imperative to repent, to believe and to be baptized (Mark 16.16; Acts 2.38; 3.19; 16.31-33). There is a commission to the Church to go forth and to baptize all nations (Matthew 28.19). For the New Testament, however, baptism is not primarily a human response, a human work or a human witness, but is a gift of God. The first Christians apparently coined a new word, *baptisma*, to distinguish this reality from human acts of ablution (*baptismoi*: Mark 7.4; Hebrews 6.2).[17] As Robinson strikingly puts it: 'The one baptism is that by which the Church is created, before it is that which the Church administers.'[18] Christ constitutes the Church by baptism, 'cleansing [or consecrating] her with the washing of water by the word' (Ephesians 5.26).

So baptism is one because Christ is one and because we are one in him. 'Baptism is one because it makes one' (J. Robinson).[19] 'By one Spirit we were all baptized into one body' (1 Corinthians 12.13). Christians are already in communion by the action of the Holy Spirit through baptism into the body of Christ. However, the reality of that communion is called into question when a church finds itself unable to acknowledge the full authenticity of another church's practice of Trinitarian baptism.

common baptism?

The theological truth of the one baptism points to the ideal of a 'common baptism', but does not create it automatically. A 'common baptism' is a baptism that is recognized across the churches, so that a person who has been baptized with water in the name of the Holy Trinity in one church, with the intention of doing what the church does, has no need to be baptized (again) when transferring his or her fellowship to another church. In fact, that person should on no account be baptized (again). Re-baptism is inconceivable, impossible, a contradiction in terms, a complete nonsense.

Behind this stance, held by Baptists and Anglicans alike, although applied in different ways, lies a theological evaluation of what baptism is and means. Baptism is seen as a gift of God that incorporates us into the community of the Church in the context of faith. It is inconceivable that this could be repeated. No one can be incorporated by the Holy Spirit into the Body of Christ more than once.[20] 'Both those who baptize infants and those who baptize only believers recognize that baptism is unrepeatable, not because we cannot repent and begin again, but because it signifies the unique action of salvation in Jesus Christ and our rebirth in him.'[21] The unique and unrepeatable nature of baptism derives from the fact that it represents sacramentally the unique saving action of God in Christ and the once for all incorporation of the Christian into that action. As Richardson says, 'the actual historical baptism of the individual Christian is important precisely in the sense in which the actual historical death of Christ is important. Both are *eph-hapax,* unrepeatable.'[22] Just as there is one Lord, one faith, one God and Father of all and one hope of our calling, so there is one baptism (Ephesians 4.4-5). Like them, it can neither be divided nor multiplied. One Christ, one cross, one sacrifice, one glorified body, one Church, one baptism.

The acknowledgement of a common baptism by churches engaged in dialogue, where this is possible, prepares the ground for further steps to unity: eucharistic hospitality; interchangeability of members and ministers; the acknowledgement of one another as authentic churches of Christ, as 'sister churches'; and a commitment to work together in mission and to overcome remaining obstacles to various stages of visible unity. Important ecumenical developments involving Anglicans have been predicated on the recognition of a baptism that is common to each of the partner churches in dialogue: e.g. the ARCIC report *Church as Communion* (1991), the Meissen Agreement (1991), the Porvoo Agreement (1996), the Reuilly Agreement (1999) and the Anglican–Methodist Covenant (2003). For Anglicans at least, the mutual recognition of baptism is a major stepping-stone to mutual recognition and commitment between churches and paves the way for a united mission.

The mutual recognition of baptism by many Christian churches has been described as an ecumenical time bomb. If you recognize their baptism, you must recognize those who are baptized as members of the Body of Christ. What judgement do you then make about the structured fellowship that they enjoy one with another? As the Second Vatican Council shows, recognition of baptism entails recognizing to some degree the ecclesial reality of those fellowships.[23] It undercuts an exclusive ecclesiology, such as the traditional Roman Catholic and Orthodox positions, which regard one's own church or communion of churches as the only true Church.

The converse also appears to be the case. Let us take a family of churches, such as the Baptist churches, that has a high valuation of baptism and relates it to its fundamental ecclesiology. This church in all conscience regards a particular practice of baptism (i.e. infant baptism) within another church as not a true baptism. It would seem to follow that the ecclesial character of the community of those so baptized is thrown in doubt. Can it be regarded as a true church (to use the language of the Reformation in both its magisterial and radical forms) or is it perhaps something less than that? Mutual affirmation and commitment (a covenantal relationship in mission and ministry) is scarcely possible.

Baptists may reply that they do indeed recognize, in some sense, these churches, though not on the basis of their baptism because they cannot recognize infant baptism as true baptism. *Believing and Being Baptized* comes close to this when it says, 'Baptists can share in a mutual recognition of others as being members of the Body of Christ, regardless of the mode of initiation in their church tradition. Being in the Body of Christ, and not baptism itself, is the basis of unity.'[24] If we ask 'How do we recognize a fellow member of the Body of Christ?' the reply is given that we recognize him or her experientially, by spiritual fruits, by the presence of the Holy Spirit, 'not by the evidence of having taken part in a particular ritual act'. There are three questions about this statement.

First: what do Baptists mean when they say that recognition of other Christians is possible for Baptists 'regardless of the mode of initiation in their church tradition'? It sounds rather cavalier about Christian initiation, as though any form or none would do. Is initiation irrelevant to mutual recognition or is it simply secondary? Perhaps the answer depends on what is meant by 'mode'. The antithesis that is played out here between 'being in the Body of Christ' and 'baptism itself' is alien to the New Testament.

Second: the phrase 'particular ritual act' raises a question. We are assured that it is meant as a neutral, descriptive term, but in its context it does seem to have overtones of mere external observance. It is played off against spiritual fruits, as though baptism were not a God-given mark of Christian identity. It seems to imply an unbiblical dichotomy between the outward sacramental action and the inward spiritual reality. However, it is only fair to say that *Believing and Being Baptized* as a whole reflects an attempt to hold the two together.

Third: if Baptists discern the reality of the Church by experiential criteria, rather than by the marks of the true Church developed by the Reformers (broadly, word, sacrament, oversight), how do they believe that the Church is constituted and what do they think is the role of means of grace in this? Is the Church constituted solely by the Holy Spirit working invisibly in the hearts and lives of believers without external means of grace? Or does the Spirit use the Word alone, without the sacraments?

Although we are told in Scripture, 'By their fruits you shall know them' (Matthew 7.20), Anglicans tend to be cautious about attempting to evaluate individuals' spiritual vitality. The classical pastoral method of Anglicanism is not to make 'windows into men's hearts and minds' (as Queen Elizabeth I famously said) or to pass judgement on their presumed spiritual state. It is rather to emphasize the importance of belonging to the visible Church, through baptism and faith, and of participating in the means of grace. It is to accept the outward profession at face value and then to challenge individuals to live up to it. Anglicans tend to start with the objective, given reality of baptism and to concentrate on pastoral ways of helping people to share in it, to live in its power day by day and to discover its riches.

It is good that many Baptists are able to recognize, on whatever grounds, other churches as belonging to the one Church of Christ, but it is unfortunate if they are not able to recognize them on those churches' own terms. For Anglicans, as for Lutherans and Reformed, the visible Church is to be recognized where 'the pure Word of God is preached, and the Sacraments be duly ministered according to Christ's ordinance' (Article XIX). It is bound to be unsatisfactory if one partner seems to say: 'I do not recognize the basis on which you believe you are a church, but I recognize you on a different basis.' Perhaps we could press our Baptist friends a little further on this point. Are Christian bodies that practise infant baptism (though they also practise believers' baptism of those who have not previously been baptized) true churches of Christ or not, as far as Baptists are concerned?

The way forward to some degree of mutual ecclesial recognition for Baptists and Anglicans may be through the development of a theology of the total process of Christian initiation. This would recognize the unique and indispensable place of baptism within an ongoing process of initiation. In addition to baptism, that process would need to include the following essential elements:

1   instruction in the faith and formation for discipleship in some kind of catechumenate;

2   a liturgical opportunity for the individual to profess the faith for themselves;

3   the laying on of hands with prayer for the confirming and strengthening power of the Holy Spirit;

4   participation in the Eucharist and reception of Holy Communion.

(The rubrics for *The Book of Common Prayer* 1662 service for 'The Ministration of Baptism to such as are of Riper Years and able to Answer for Themselves', echoed in Canon B24, stress that examination and instruction of the candidates shall take place in good time and that they shall be exhorted to prepare themselves by prayer and fasting to receive this sacrament.)

As far as Anglicans are concerned there are two important conditions that would need to be built into any such mutual recognition of a total process of Christian initiation.

First, it could not imply any defect in the baptism of infants that would somehow be rectified by putting in place the other elements of the process of Christian initiation. There could be no suggestion that infant baptism was not a true baptism at the time, but could subsequently become recognized as such when supplemented by catechesis, profession of faith, confirmation and Holy Communion. Anglicans could not accept any additional criteria for authentic baptism than the classical criteria of catholic theology: that baptism should be in water, in the triune Name, and with the intention of doing what the Church does. The integrity of the baptism administered to infants could not be impugned, though that would not imply that it comprised complete Christian initiation. In other words, it would have to be seen as complete as baptism (and therefore not to be repeated), though not complete as Christian initiation.

Second, any agreement for the mutual recognition of a total process of Christian initiation would have to rule out the (re-)baptism of those who had been baptized in infancy, on the understanding that the other vital elements of Christian initiation set this in a fresh light. Anglicans would only be able to recognizea total pattern of Christian initiation if it excluded in principle *second* baptism. Comparability of processes of initiation could not accommodate what Anglicans would regard as re-baptism. (In that connection, Anglicans should be aware that 'open membership' Baptist congregations do not insist on (re-)baptism.) Given that assurance, it is likely that Anglicans in turn could recognize the pattern of Christian initiation that involves believers' baptism of those who had not previously undergone trinitarian baptism. After all, this is fully provided for and takes place routinely in the Church of England.

To bring about this reciprocity in baptismal policy would, I think, involve some kind of 'economy' (in the Patristic sense) or 'accommodation' (as the Reformers used to say) for both Anglicans and Baptists. This would mean that both Anglicans and Baptists were making some allowance and not insisting that the other tradition should do things exactly as they would themselves. Baptists would not be endorsing infant baptism, but they would be acknowledging that, when seen within the total process of initiation, it could be accommodated. Anglicans would not be giving up their conviction that (as the Thirty-nine Articles put it) 'the Baptism of young Children is in any wise to be retained in the Church, as most agreeable with the institution of Christ,' but they would be acknowledging that the pattern of initiation practised by those who do not share this conviction was authentic as Christian initiation. This mutual authentication of two patterns of Christian initiation that are not completely identical would seem to be an essential prerequisite for Anglicans and Baptists being able to see the Church of Jesus Christ in each other's churches.

one baptism: summary and questions to the churches

Baptism has an essential place within the whole process of initiation, which is the journey of Christian beginnings. Baptism, understood in this way, is a sharing in the one baptism which is the life, death and resurrection of Jesus Christ. Anglicans and Baptists can thus recognize in each other that they have truly made a journey through the beginning of the Christian life. The baptism of children gives joy to Anglicans, and Baptists feel deeply that in the baptism of believers they have a great treasure. Pain is caused to Anglicans when a Baptist church baptizes as a believer someone previously baptized as an infant. Pain is also caused to people in Baptist churches who forgo the baptism as a believer which they desire, for the sake of healing wounds within the wider Church. We therefore offer these challenges to our two traditions:

1   Could the member churches of the Baptist Union of Great Britain reflect on the nature of Christian initiation as a process, and consider whether they might recognize a place for the baptism of infants within the whole journey which marks the beginning of the Christian life? This question is asked in the context of an Anglican understanding that the beginning has not come to an end until Christian disciples confess faith in Christ as Lord for themselves and are commissioned for service in the Church and world.

2   Will member churches of the Baptist Union of Great Britain which practise open membership resolve that, where they agree to a request for a second baptism, it should only be after careful pastoral counselling of enquirers? In such a conversation, enquirers would be made fully aware of alternative paths within the journey of initiation.

3   Would the Council of the Baptist Union of Great Britain appoint a group to prepare a service of worship which might offer a form in which those baptized as infants, but not yet confirmed, can mark their public profession of faith and reception of spiritual gifts in some other way than baptism?

4   Could member churches of the Baptist Union of Great Britain adopt the policy that those who have never received the sign of baptism, whether as an infant or as a believer,

should not be admitted to membership without being baptized?

5   Could the Council of the Baptist Union of Great Britain invite Baptist churches which are part of single-congregation LEPs to refrain from baptizing as a believer those who have previously been baptized as infants?

6   Where individual Anglicans have received a second baptism in a Baptist church, will parish churches within the Church of England nevertheless continue to welcome them as full participants in their life?

7   In a situation where a Baptist church follows the recommendation outlined in point two above, will a parish of the Church of England refuse to allow the practice of second baptism to disrupt their partnership in life and mission with Baptists there?

8   In the light of the whole process of Christian initiation described in this report, will all parishes in the Church of England pastorally support those parents who believe it is right to defer the baptism of their children until they reach the age of discretion?

9   Could all parishes reflect on the consistent teaching of the Church of England that infants are baptized on the understanding that they will receive Christian nurture, with the intention that they will come to confirmation and so profess the faith for themselves?

10   Can the Church of England and Baptist churches determine that neither differences in baptismal practice nor the situation of second baptisms should prevent them from seeing in each other the presence of the one true Church of Jesus Christ?

mutual recognition?
towards a common life

chapter six

oversight and continuity

At first glance it might seem that Baptists and Anglicans are poles apart when it comes to how the church is governed and how pastoral oversight is exercised. Their structures are strikingly different, and yet on closer inspection the principles underlying them have much in common.

structures of oversight within the Baptist tradition

The Baptists of the seventeenth century were convinced of the need to reorder the church according to what they saw reflected in the biblical accounts. They rejected the episcopal system, and the need for 'authorization' from anywhere outside the local church in order to exist.

When thinking about the Church, the starting point and central idea for Baptists has always been the presence of Christ in the local congregation, where believers gather in covenant under his rule to seek to know his mind. The fellowship of believers is thereby endowed with the privileges of God's covenant of grace, including the ministry of word and sacrament, without further sanction from an external ecclesiastical authority.

This does not of course mean that each local congregation is entirely independent and cut off from a wider community – nor that ministry belongs only in the local congregation. While it is true that the main focus of ministry and energy is local, the conviction that each church is in relationship with 'the other baptized churches' was present from the earliest stages of Baptist life. This can be seen in the letters exchanged between congregations, the drawing up of 'agreed' confessions of faith, and the meeting of representatives of the churches in 'associations' on a regional basis for mutual encouragement and counsel. Those who ministered in these congregations did so on the basis of the call of God and the recognition of the congregation, rather than because of a 'licensing' or ordaining by a civil–religious hierarchy. This did not mean that the early Baptists, either General or

Particular, regarded ministry as unimportant or as self-generated. Ministry was one of God's gifts to the people of God, and to be honoured and exercised as such.

Even though the main focus for ministry in the Baptist tradition has always been the local church, in which pastors (also called 'elders' or 'bishops') and deacons were appointed from the very beginning, we also find references from early on to those who were called messengers.

The first mention we find is from the seventeenth century in the Hexham records,[1] in which one Thomas Tillam is referred to as being a 'messenger of one of the seven London churches'. He appears to be sent from one of the metropolitan congregations into Northumberland, Cheshire and Yorkshire as a travelling evangelist. Other references to a similar pattern are present. Members in various congregations, particularly in the London churches, having given evidence of an evangelistic gift, were specially commissioned to travel to specific places to preach and establish congregations. Each journey would have its particular commissioning and, for the duration of that journey, the individual would be recognized as a 'messenger' – a designation that seems to have ceased at the end of the trip. Eventually, those who clearly had a continuing call to this ministry were recognized as messengers in a more general sense, and the ministry was recognized as ongoing. Representatives 'sent' from the local church to meet in associations of churches could also be called 'messengers', but the title is of particular interest in being applied to those 'sent' to exercise a pastoral ministry within a context of mission.

The missionary focus in the early examples of messengers is echoed in the renewed emphasis that is being placed today on the apostolic, missionary, and church-planting nature of ministry which is exercised beyond the boundaries of the local congregation ('trans-local' ministry). This stands in some contrast to the aspects of pastoral care, administration, good order and maintenance which occupied the centre of Baptist trans-local ministry, mostly focused in the work of 'general superintendents', during almost the whole of the last century. Notwithstanding this perceptible shift in emphasis, there is wide recognition that mission and pastoral care both belong to the ministry of oversight; and that the exercising of oversight is based on covenant relationships between the regional minister and other ministers, with their local churches, their associations, and also with the council and assembly of the Union.

The report issued to the Baptist Union of Great Britain Council in the late 1990s entitled *Relating and Resourcing*[2] proposed a radical recasting of the life of the Union, in which constitutional and institutional expressions would be replaced by another language, logic and ethos which was altogether more relational, covenantal and mission-intentional. The report noted that 'the church is a movement of God rather than an institution of our making'. Institutions are not to be devalued but they are to be kept flexible in order to serve the purpose of this moment rather than the past one. So, for example, Baptists do not regard the three-fold order of ministry as a timeless unchanging institution. Ministry evolves in ways appropriate to different times and contexts.

In response to the challenges facing the church at the start of the twenty-first century this report recommended that the churches of the Union relate together within and across twelve regional associations rather than the former twenty-nine associations. Moreover, it recommended that the leadership and oversight within associations should be transferred from general superintendents to regional ministry teams.

The implementation of these recommendations has now been completed, and it is clear that the changes have strengthened the prevailing view that the primary role of regional ministers (formerly superintendents) must be that of leaders in mission, and moreover this responsibility should be shared by a team, not vested in one person.

structures of oversight within the Anglican tradition

Anglican parishes are grouped in dioceses led by bishops; and beyond the diocese there is the province or national church. The parish priest shares the ministry of word and sacrament, pastoral care and oversight with the diocesan bishop as the chief pastor and father in God of all in the diocese (Canon C 18).[3] In his formal oversight of the diocese the bishop administers the corporate policy and discipline of the church, embodied in its canons. In this he is assisted by suffragan bishops, archdeacons and rural deans and consults with the Bishop's Council.

However, it would not be correct to think of Anglicanism as simply hierarchical and clerical in its governance. For instance, in the Church of England, at every level of the church's life there is responsible involvement by lay people: from the annual parochial church meeting, which elects the Parochial Church Council, through deanery and diocesan synods, to the General Synod with its three houses of bishops, clergy and laity. The diocesan synod has overall responsibility for the policy and budget of the diocese; diocesan committees and boards are appointed by the synod and are answerable to it. At the national level, major policy decisions require consultation with dioceses before the General Synod votes by houses. No significant change of policy can happen without the consent of all three houses. While the bishops have a special responsibility to give a lead to the church in the three areas of doctrine, worship and ministry, they have to carry the clergy and laity with them.

theological convergence

In spite of the very different structures of oversight arising from quite distinct ecclesiologies, some surprising common ground can be discovered if we look beneath the surface of church structures and ask about the deep theological rationale for how Baptist and Anglican Churches conduct themselves. In both traditions we find a concern for faithfulness to the apostolic foundation of the Church and its apostolic mission (apostolicity) and for sharing together as a community in the life of God the Holy Trinity through grace (*koinonia*). Participation in the apostolic mission and the means of grace is a theme that links both Anglican and Baptist understandings of oversight.

Richard Hooker, a foundational interpreter of the Church of England's ecclesiology who died in 1600, used the ancient Christian concept of mutual participation or co-inherence (*perichoresis*) as a key to the doctrine of grace and the Church.[4] Christ and the Church, his body, indwell each other. Christians share in him and in salvation as they are joined in community to each other. For Hooker, such participation (which resonates with the New Testament concept of *koinonia*) is much more than mere association while not being a complete loss of distinct identity. It is a two-way relationship of giving and receiving. Hooker then employs the idea of participation to defend the co-inherence, but not simple identity, of Church and State in a way that has shaped the Anglican ethos in England through the centuries. While the application of the notion of co-inherence to the relation between Church and

State was opposed to 'Separatist' convictions, Hooker's emphasis on mutual participation at the heart of church life has strong similarities to the Baptist tradition.

In the thought of such early Baptists as John Smyth, a contemporary of Richard Hooker, the eternal covenant of grace is actualized in the covenant commitment of the local church.[5] The covenant made within the Trinity for accomplishing human salvation is made real in history as disciples promise to walk together and watch over each other under the rule of Christ. This *koinonia* extends beyond the local church as particular congregations meet together in association. Baptist ecclesiology has always aspired to withstand individualism, recognizing the interdependence of communities of faith, since local congregations all 'walk by the same rule . . . as members of one body in the common faith under Christ their only head'.[6]

At the time of the Reformation, Anglicans used the term 'congregation' to refer to the universal Church (Article XIX; Homily for Whitsunday). Many Anglicans today would refer colloquially to the local worshipping community as 'the congregation' or 'the local church', but the Church of England's polity thinks formally in terms of the community of the parish, rather than the gathered congregation, and regards the diocese as the local church, the locus of the bishop's superintending ministry in the areas of word, sacrament and pastoral care.

For both Anglicans and Baptists, therefore, participation in the *koinonia* of the triune God creates community in different spheres of church and inter-church life. This in turn calls for pastoral oversight, the ministry of *episkope* that fosters *koinonia*. Theological dialogues, including that which resulted in *Baptism, Eucharist and Ministry*, have devoted much attention to the question of the ministry of *episkope* or oversight. Baptists and Anglicans agree that a ministry of pastoral responsibility is necessary to safeguard the unity of the Church and to serve its mission, though the particular form of that ministry differs in our two traditions.

At the Reformation, the Church of England continued the ministry of oversight exercised by bishops both locally, in the diocese, and collectively, in the episcopal college. In the diocese, which is for Anglicans ecclesiologically the local church, the bishop provides pastoral leadership in mission (the 1980 Ordinal says that he is to promote the Church's mission throughout the world).[7] This mission embraces the ministry of word and sacrament, worship, doctrine and discipline. The 1980 Ordinal also says: 'A bishop is called to lead in serving and caring for the people of God and to work with them in the oversight of the Church.' This highlights the relational and corporate character of the ministry of oversight in the Church of England. Those called to exercise oversight in the Church cannot fulfil their responsibility without collaboration with clergy and laity.

In the Church of England and the wider Anglican Communion oversight is exercised at every level of the Church's life in the three dimensions that *Baptism, Eucharist and Ministry* describes as personal, collegial and communal. Bishops exercise oversight in a personal way in their dioceses. In the House of Bishops they exercise oversight collegially. With clergy and laity in synods they exercise the ministry of oversight in a communal way. These same dimensions of the ministry of oversight are reflected at the diocesan, provincial, national and world levels in the Anglican Communion. The bishops have recently done work on episcopal collegiality[8] and on the ministry of suffragan bishops who share in the episcopal ministry of oversight.

Baptists also recognize personal, collegial and communal dimensions of oversight, though they view these in a rather different context. The basic personal ministry of oversight is given to the minister or pastor in the local church, whom some early Baptists called bishop. This is comparable to the Anglican understanding of the ministry of the bishop in the diocese, except that the local church in which the Baptist 'bishop' ministers comprises one or two local congregations (cf. the Anglican rector or vicar). Oversight in the congregation flows to and fro between the personal and the communal, since the responsibility of 'watching over' the church belongs to all the members gathered in Church Meeting and to the pastor. Baptists thus have a two-fold office, rather than a three-fold order of ministry: *episkope* and *diakonia*. Team ministry in a local church, between ministers and deacons (and/or elders), gives scope for the collegial dimension of *episkope* in the local scene.

Baptists also recognize *episkope* at an inter-church level. Oversight is exercised communally by the regional association of churches, which in assembly seeks the mind of Christ for the life and mission of the member churches, while having no power to impose decisions on the local Church Meeting. Oversight flows between the communal, personal and collegial here too. Personal oversight is exercised by various 'association ministers' – regional ministers. The inter-church ministry of the regional minister is certainly understood to be episcopal, in the sense of being a form of pastoral oversight, but this is seen as an extension of the episcopal ministry of the local pastor; the difference is one of the scope of exercise of the *episkope* rather than a difference of order.[9] Regional ministers also work collegially with each other and in partnership with various officers of the Baptist Union of Great Britain. In principle Baptists recognize the same flow between communal, collegial and personal forms of *episkope* at the national level of the Union of churches. This principle is set out in a discussion document: *The Nature of the Assembly and the Council of the Baptist Union of Great Britain.*[10]

It is clear that in recent years both Baptists and Anglicans have been seeking to discover how the ministry of *episkope* can be more effectively actualized at various levels of church life. As *Baptism, Eucharist and Ministry* points out, in various churches one or another of these dimensions has been overemphasized at the expense of others and a corrective needs to be applied.

> In some churches, the personal dimension of the ordained ministry tends to diminish the collegial and communal dimensions. In other churches, the collegial or communal dimension takes so much importance that the ordained ministry loses its personal dimension. Each church needs to ask itself in what way its exercise of ordained ministry has suffered in the course of history.[11]

the issue of continuity

One of the issues that has seemed to divide Anglicans and Baptists has been that of how apostolicity is expressed and maintained. The Anglican tradition has been marked by a strong concern to maintain visible continuity with the tradition of the Church and its faith, going back through the changes of the Reformation, the medieval church and Celtic Christianity to the early Fathers and ultimately to the apostles themselves. The Church of England affirms that it stands in continuity, through ministry in its parishes and sees (dioceses), with the immediately pre-Reformation church in England. Correspondingly, it has responded to separation from itself by challenging dissenters with the question of their own visible continuity. Generally, however, Baptists have not been particularly concerned with establishing apostolic continuity in a linear sense. Rather, they have seen faithfulness to the witness of the Apostles as one of the marks of the Church. The continuity of apostolic faith was indeed also the primary concern of the English Reformers – issues of visible continuity became important to Anglicans at a later period.

In the Church of England, the question of apostolic continuity has been freshly explored in *The Porvoo Common Statement,*[12] which itself builds on the description of apostolicity in *Baptism, Eucharist and Ministry.* In *The Porvoo Common Statement*, three aspects of apostolicity are identified.

- The primary manifestation of apostolic succession is to be found in the Church as a whole, as it participates in the mission of Jesus and is faithful to 'the words and acts of Jesus transmitted by the Apostles'. This means that Anglicans are able to recognize, at a formal level, churches that are not episcopally ordered as sharing in the apostolic mission of the whole people of God.

- This continuity is served by the ministry of word, sacrament and pastoral oversight within the Church. It follows that Anglicans are able to recognize formally the authenticity of such a ministry even when it is not incorporated into the episcopal succession.

- The continuous ordination of bishops, to whom is committed the ordination of other ministers, is a 'sign' of apostolic continuity. Anglicans are able to distinguish, as *Baptism, Eucharist and Ministry* does, between the sign and the reality of apostolic continuity, and to recognize the reality even in the absence of the sign. Since faithfulness to the apostolic calling of the whole Church can be carried by more than one means, those churches that have not used the sign of the historic episcopate might henceforth embrace it, for the sake of greater unity and enhanced communion, without any adverse judgement on their past ministry.

A Baptist approach to apostolic continuity will certainly be in accord with the first two aspects, which are in fact explicitly affirmed in the recent Baptist Union of Great Britain discussion document *Forms of Ministry Among Baptists*.[13] Further, the continuity in faithfulness of the whole church is expressed in the assemblies of the church, at both association and local level. In particular, Baptists find continuity in the Church Meeting, whose decisions over the years are recorded in the Church Book; so the current generation acknowledges that it is part of the story of God's faithful people in that place in the past, who have themselves aimed to stand in the succession of the early Church.

Baptists will have more difficulty with the third aspect, even given the flexibility of this approach. Baptists will note that even where it is not possible to establish conclusively a linear succession of bishops, the Porvoo statement proposes that the sign is meaningful and effective when the church formally 'intends' to have a historic succession from the apostles: 'To ordain a bishop in historic succession, that is in intended continuity from the Apostles themselves, is also a sign.'[14] What matters in Porvoo is the intention, and commitment to this intention, not just the way it has been realized in the accidents of history. Baptists might then wonder why this should be a necessary sign, given the fact that apostolic continuity resides in the whole Church and in its ministry. They should note, however, that there is a prior assumption in the tradition of the Church of England that leads it to insist on the sign of episcopal continuity for the full visible unity of the one Church. That is the conviction that there is a distinct order of ministry (bishop), inherited from the earliest days of the Church, which is given oversight of the other two (presbyter and deacon), while sharing it with them, and that ordination is an expression of that ministry of oversight.

While ordination of presbyters and deacons by the bishop is thus essential for the health of the Church according to the Church of England, among Baptists the presiding of a regional minister at an ordination is usually regarded as 'good order' rather than essential. Baptists, however, do more generally require the gathering of other churches and their ministers to offer their consent for ordination and be involved in the act, since the local minister represents the wider Church of Christ to the local community.

conclusion

Despite the differences in structure and theology, there is a growing convergence in theological reflections on ministry and oversight. This offers the hope that it might be possible to recognize the authenticity of each other's forms of ministry in the same way as recognizing each other's processes of initiation into the Christian life: that is, within the concept of a common pattern rather than looking for symmetry in structures and practice.

chapter seven

apostolicity and recognition: an Anglican contribution

introduction

This chapter sets out to do three things. First, to explore the meaning of the term 'apostolicity'. Second, to explain the Church of England's position on what it means to see another church as 'apostolic', using the Reuilly agreement between the British and Irish Anglican Churches and the French Lutheran and Reformed Churches as an example. Third, in the light of this position, to consider whether, and if so how, it would be possible for the Church of England to discern the mark of apostolicity in the churches of the Baptist Union of Great Britain.

the meaning of apostolicity

In common with other Christians around the world, Christians in the Church of England affirm in the words of the Nicene Creed that they believe in 'One, Holy, Catholic and Apostolic Church'. Canon A 1 of the *Canons of the Church of England*[1] also makes it clear that the Church of England believes that it is part of this apostolic church:

> The Church of England, established according to the laws of this realm under the Queen's Majesty, belongs to the true and apostolic church of Christ; and, as our duty to the said Church of England requires, we do constitute and ordain that no member thereof shall be at liberty to maintain or hold the contrary.

The question that is raised by these statements in the Creed and the Canons is what is meant by the term 'apostolic'. In order to understand what we mean by this term we need to begin by noting that the root of the English word 'apostolic' is the Greek verb *apostello*, which means to send. Building on this, we can say that the Church is apostolic because it is has been sent by Christ just as he himself was sent by God the Father.

In the Bible we find from Moses onwards a whole series of prophetic messengers sent by God to declare his will and his promises to his people and to the world. As Alan Richardson puts it, God's

> characteristic approach to men is by sending someone to speak to them for him: he sends Moses to Pharaoh, Nathan to David, Elijah to Ahab, Amos to Bethel, Isaiah to Hezekiah, and so on almost indefinitely. 'Since the day that your fathers came forth out of the land of Egypt unto this day, I have sent unto you all my servants the prophets, daily rising up early and sending them' (Jeremiah 7.25; cf. 26.5, 29.19; 35.15; 44.4).[2]

In the New Testament this pattern of sending reaches its climax in the sending of Jesus Christ (Mark 12.1-12). He is seen as the eschatological prophet predicted by Moses in Deuteronomy 18.15 (see Acts 3.22), the one who definitively reveals God to the world because as God the Son he shares the divine nature (John 1.1-18, Hebrews 1.1-3).

It is this understanding of who Christ is that is reflected in the description of him as 'the apostle and high priest of our confession' in Hebrews 3.1. As F. F. Bruce puts it in his commentary on Hebrews, the writer to the Hebrews calls Christ 'apostle' in this verse because he is 'the one in whom God has revealed himself finally and completely'.[3]

What we also find in the New Testament is that Christ gathers around himself a group of people, the apostles, who are called to share his mission of making God known. Thus we read in Mark 3.13-15:

> He went up the mountain and called to him those whom he wanted, and they came to him. And he appointed twelve, whom he also named apostles, to be with him, and to be sent out to proclaim the message, and to have authority to cast out demons.

In verse 15, as in the Gospels as a whole, the casting out of demons is an integral part of making God known because it reveals God as the one who has authority over the powers of evil.

In addition, we are told that the apostles and a wider group of disciples with them were commissioned to continue Christ's mission on earth in the power of the Holy Spirit after his resurrection and ascension:

> And Jesus came and said to them, 'All authority in heaven and on earth has been given to me. Go therefore and make disciples of all nations, baptizing them in the name of the Father and of the Son and of the Holy Spirit, and teaching them to obey everything that I have commanded you. And remember, I am with you always, to the end of the age.' (Matthew 28.18-20)

> Jesus said to them again, 'Peace be with you. As the Father has sent me, so I send you.' When he had said this, he breathed on them and said to them, 'Receive the Holy Spirit. If you forgive the sins of any they are forgiven them, if you retain the sins of any, they are retained.' (John 20.21-23)

> But you will receive power when the Holy Spirit has come upon you; and you shall be my witnesses in Jerusalem, in all Judea and Samaria, and to the ends of the earth. (Acts 1.8)

> Paul, a servant of Jesus Christ, called to be an apostle, set apart for the gospel of God, which he promised beforehand through his prophets in the holy scriptures, the gospel concerning his Son, who was descended from David according to the flesh and was declared to be Son of God with power according to the Spirit of holiness by resurrection from the dead, Jesus Christ our Lord, through whom we have received grace and apostleship to bring about the obedience of faith among all the Gentiles for the sake of his name, including yourselves who are called to belong to Jesus Christ. (Romans 1.1-6)

From these texts we can see that the apostles were those who were called by the risen Christ to proclaim the gospel and to bring about the obedience of faith among all the nations. It follows, therefore, that when we say that the Church is apostolic we mean two things: first, it is a community in which the gospel preached by the apostles is believed and lived out in the obedience of faith in the power of the Spirit; second, it is a community which is summoned by the risen Christ to go on proclaiming that same gospel among all nations in the power of the Spirit so that people who are not yet believers will enter into the obedience of faith.

In the words of the Church of England House of Bishops report, *Apostolicity and Succession*:

> The Church can be described as apostolic in two principal senses: on the one hand, it is historically founded and still rests upon the apostles Jesus sent and their witness to him. On the other hand it is itself 'apostled' or 'sent' in every generation. This means that it is dynamic in its mission and that its continuity is filled with God's purpose for the world and looks beyond history to eternity, the *eschaton*.[4]

The reference to the mission of the Church looking beyond history to eternity makes the point that the gospel that the Church is summoned to believe and to proclaim is concerned with how God's eternal kingdom has begun to break into our world through the life, death and resurrection of Christ, and that the obedience of faith means living appropriately in the light of this fact.

how the Church of England has understood the apostolicity of particular churches

If this is what it means for the Christian Church as a whole to be 'apostolic', it follows that to say that any particular Christian church is apostolic means that it too shares these characteristics of apostolicity. The question then becomes: How are these characteristics manifested in a particular church in such a way that we can say it is 'apostolic'?

At the time of the Reformation the English Reformers followed the theologians of the Lutheran Reformation[5] by defining the basic characteristics of a particular, visible, apostolic church as follows:

> The visible Church of Christ is a congregation of faithful men, in which the pure Word of God is preached, and the Sacraments be duly ministered according to Christ's ordinance in all those things that of necessity are requisite and necessary to the same. (Thirty-nine Articles, XIX)

If we look further at this definition we can see that it is concerned with the right proclamation of the gospel through the preaching of the word and the ministration of the sacraments so that people may enter into, and be built up in, the obedience of faith.

According to the Anglican Reformers a church that does these things is a true apostolic church and conversely a church that does not is not. It was on this basis, by applying these criteria, that the Church of England was willing to recognize the continental Lutheran and Reformed churches as true churches.[6]

There are four important points that need to be noted about Article XIX if it is to be properly understood. First, in the sixteenth century the word congregation did not have same meaning as it has today. Today we use it to describe a group of people gathered together for worship. In the sixteenth century it was simply used to describe a group of people regardless of the size of the group and regardless of whether or not they were gathered together in one place. What this means is that Article XIX cannot be used to support the idea that the English Reformers believed in a congregational form of church polity. To quote Kevin Giles:

> To argue that article 19 defines the church as a local congregation and no more is a profound mistake. To do so is to read the word 'congregation' in this context anachronistically. Such an understanding of the church by any of the Reformers is untenable. The use of congregation to refer to the whole Christian community is common in this period. For example, Bishop Hooper writes, 'I believe and confess one catholic and universal church, which is an holy congregation, an assembly of all faithful believers.' While in the Belgic confession, the affirmation is: 'we believe and confess one catholic or universal church, which is the holy *congregation* of true believers' (art. 27). This usage is also seen in the Authorized version of 1611, where 'congregation' is used to translate the Hebrew word *edah*, meaning all Israel, the covenant community.[7]

In Article XIX the word congregation is used in the same sense in which it is used by Hooper and the Belgic Confession. It refers to the universal church of which particular churches, such as the Church of England, are the local expression.

Second, the preaching of the pure Word of God, though it included the preaching of justification by grace alone through faith alone, was not exhausted by it. As we can see from Articles I–XVIII and from other authorized accounts of the theology of the reformed Church of England, such as John Jewel's *An Apology for the Church of England* or Alexander Nowell's *Catechism*,[8] what counted as the necessary content of sound preaching was an Augustinian version of the Patristic reading of the biblical witness. That is why the Thirty-nine Articles not only emphasize Trinitarian and Christological orthodoxy (see Articles I–V and VIII) but also include articles on predestination and original sin (Articles IX and XVII). It was because the continental Lutheran and Reformed churches also accepted this understanding of the nature of Christian orthodoxy that the English reformers were able to recognize them as true apostolic churches. Conversely, radical Protestant groups who showed their unwillingness to accept it by questioning, for example, Trinitarian or Christological orthodoxy and the doctrines of original sin and predestination, were regarded as heretical sects who had departed from the Church of Christ.[9] What this means is that at the time of the Reformation the Church of England was committed to a comprehensive understanding of Christian orthodoxy as the basis for ecclesial recognition, and, as we shall see, this continues to be the case today.

Third, infant baptism was included among the things that went to make up the due ministration of the sacraments. At the time of the Reformation, as today, there were those who argued against infant baptism, but the Church of England continued to maintain the theological integrity of the practice. In the words of Nowell:

> Sith it is certain that our infants have the force, and as it were the substance of baptism common with us they have wrong done them if the sign, which is inferior to the truth itself, should be denied them; and the same, which greatly availeth to testifying of the mercy of God and confirming his promises being taken away, Christians should be defrauded of a singular comfort which they that were in old time enjoyed, and so should our infants be more hardly dealt with in the New Testament under Christ, than was dealt with the Jew's infants in the Old Testament under Moses. Therefore most great reason it is that by baptism, as by the print of a seal, it be assured to our infants that they be heirs of God's grace, and of the salvation promised to the seed of the faithful.[10]

Because it took this view of the matter, the post-Reformation Church of England refused to give recognition as true Christian churches to those Christian groups which rejected infant baptism, and this issue is still something that the Church of England would have to address if it were to consider giving formal recognition to churches of a Baptist persuasion.

Fourth, the belief that the sacraments should be rightly ministered included a belief that they should be ministered by those who were properly authorized to do so. To quote Nowell again:

Sith the duties and offices of feeding the Lord's flock with God's word and the ministering of sacraments, are most nearly joined together, there is no doubt that the ministration thereof properly belongeth to them to whom the office of public teaching is committed. For as the Lord himself at his supper, exercising the authority of the public minister, did set forth his own example to be followed, so did he commit the offices of baptizing and teaching peculiarly to his apostles.[11]

Nowell's reference in the last line of this quotation to Our Lord committing the ministerial office to the apostles then raises the question 'To whom did the apostles in turn commit it?' As is well known, the answer that the Church of England gave to this question is set out in the famous opening words of the Preface to the Ordinal attached to *The Book of Common Prayer*:

It is evident unto all men diligently reading holy Scripture and ancient Authors, that from the Apostles' time there have been these Orders of Ministers in Christ's Church; Bishops, Priests, and Deacons.

These words declare that the Church of England believes that the evidence that exists points to the fact that the ordained ministry of the Christian Church has a distinctive form that has been constant since apostolic times and in this sense may be described as 'apostolic'.[12] Furthermore, because this is the case, the Preface goes on to say that the Church of England holds that it is important that 'these Orders may be continued, and reverently used and esteemed' and the Ordinal is intended to ensure that this will be the case. As Stephen Neill puts it:

In many things the Church of England may be accused of ambiguity; these sentences are marked by a superb lucidity, and leave no doubt at all that the intention of their authors, and of those who used this service, was to continue in the Church of England those orders of bishop, priest, and deacon which had existed in the Church since the time of the Apostles, *and no others*.[13]

As it is also well known, the English Reformers were not inclined to doubt the validity of the ordained ministries of the continental reformed churches simply because they did not conform to the traditional order. Thus we find Richard Hooker declaring in *Of the Laws of Ecclesiastical Polity*:

> For mine own part, although I see that certain reformed churches, the Scottish especially and the French, have not that which best agreeth with the sacred Scripture, I mean the government that is by bishops . . . this their defect and imperfection I had rather lament in such case than exagitate [i.e. censure], considering that men oftentimes, without any fault of their own, may be driven to want that kind of polity or regiment that is best.[14]

However, this did not mean that the Church of England took the traditional apostolic ordering of the ministry lightly. On the contrary, throughout the sixteenth and seventeenth centuries it insisted that it should be maintained in the face of pressure from the radical Puritans for its abolition, and indeed came to insist more firmly on its importance in the face of this pressure.[15]

In the eighteenth century a number of Anglican theologians emphasized the importance of episcopacy as a sign of the Church's separate identity over and against the State:

> High Church clergy who refused the oath to William III began making claims for episcopacy, this time not over against the Reformed, but over against political power. Episcopacy is a divine gift and in the apostolic office of a bishop lay the Church's authority and identity – independent of Parliament. The succession of bishops was emphasized in continuity with the Apostolic office. The Church's constitution is independent of that of civil society and only by maintaining that constitution – ordination by persons standing in succession to the Apostles – can the Church maintain its identity.[16]

A similar point was also made in the following century by the early Tractarians. Faced with what they saw as the increasing religious indifference of the state, the Tractarians, like their eighteenth-century predecessors, argued that the authority of the Church was not based on the support it received from the temporal power but on its apostolic descent by reason of unbroken episcopal succession. As the first of the *Tracts for the Times* declared:

> Christ has not left his church without claims of its own upon the attention of men. Surely not. Hard Master He cannot be, to bid us oppose the world, yet give us no credentials for so doing. There are some who rest their divine mission on their own unsupported assertion; others who rest it upon their popularity; others on their success; and others who rest it upon their temporal distinctions. This last case has, perhaps, been too much our own; I fear that we have neglected the real ground on which our authority is built, – OUR APOSTOLICAL DESCENT.[17]

In summary, what we find in the normative Anglican documents that emerged from the English Reformation is a dual position. On the one hand, Anglicans are able to recognize other churches, which do not have the traditional three-fold ministerial order, as genuinely apostolic, on the grounds that in them the word is rightly preached and the sacraments are rightly ministered by a ministry exercising oversight. On the other hand, there is a firm belief that the traditional Catholic three-fold ministry is apostolic in origin and therefore ought to be maintained.

What has happened in the centuries since is that some Church of England theologians, particularly those from the Protestant and evangelical wing of the church, have emphasized that part of the traditional Anglican position which gave recognition to non-episcopal churches and their ministerial orders, while others from the church's catholic wing have emphasized that part of the traditional Anglican position which insisted on the normative nature of the three-fold pattern of ministry and as a result have questioned the apostolicity of these churches and their orders.[18]

apostolicity and recognition in *The Reuilly Common Statement*

If we fast-forward the film to today, we see that the current Church of England ecumenical approach combines elements of both the approaches that have just been outlined, together with the influence of wider ecumenical thinking about these matters. A helpful illustration of this approach is provided by *The Reuilly Common Statement* of 1999, which records the ecumenical agreement reached by the British and Irish Anglican Churches and the French Lutheran and Reformed Churches. The reason why this statement is helpful for our concerns is because the French Reformed Churches are the closest to the Baptist Union of Great Britain in terms of traditions and polity of any of the Church of England's current ecumenical partners. In this statement we find three significant elements.

First, we find the Church of England giving unequivocal recognition to four non-episcopal churches:[19]

> We acknowledge one another's churches as churches belonging to the One, Holy, Catholic and Apostolic Church of Jesus Christ and truly participating in the apostolic mission of the whole people of God.[20]

If we ask why it is that this acknowledgement can be made, the answer is that it is dependent on three further acknowledgements which correspond to the classic criteria for recognition identified at the Reformation:

> We acknowledge that in all our churches the word of God is authentically preached, and the sacraments of baptism and the Eucharist are duly administered.

> We acknowledge that all our churches share in the common confession of the apostolic faith.

> We acknowledge that one another's ordained ministries are given by God as instruments of grace for the mission and unity of the Church and for the proclamation of the word and the celebration of the sacraments.[21]

In accordance with the Reformation commitment to comprehensive theological orthodoxy noted above, the acknowledgement of a 'common confession of the apostolic faith' is based on a chapter entitled 'Agreement in Faith' which records specified 'agreements in faith' (drawing on other contemporary ecumenical texts) on a whole range of key theological loci, ranging from agreement on the authority of Scripture[22] to eschatological hope and its ethical consequences.[23] These agreements in faith also include agreed statements about baptism and the Eucharist. This is important because it means that the acknowledgement that in all the churches involved the sacraments are duly administered is based on a shared understanding of the nature of these sacraments.

Second, we find a mutual acknowledgement of the ecclesial nature of these churches' ministries, which from the Anglican side reflects the classic balance of the sixteenth-century Anglican Reformers by affirming the authenticity of non-episcopal ministries while still insisting on the abiding significance of the historic episcopate. Thus the chapter on 'The Apostolicity of the Church and Ministry' declares that all parties to the statement agree that:

> Within the apostolicity of the whole Church is an apostolic succession of the ministry which serves, and is a focus of, the continuity of the Church in its life in Christ and its faithfulness to the words and acts of Jesus transmitted by the apostles. The ordained ministry has a particular responsibility for witnessing to this apostolic tradition and for proclaiming it afresh with authority in every generation.[24]

The chapter then goes on to set out the agreements and differences on ministry between the Anglican tradition on the one hand and the Lutheran and Reformed traditions on the other.

> Anglicans believe that the historic episcopate is a sign of the apostolicity of the whole Church. The ordination of a bishop in historic succession (that is, in intended continuity with the apostles themselves) is a sign of God's promise to be with the Church, and also the way the Church communicates its care for the continuity in the whole of its faith, life and mission, and renews its intention and determination to manifest the permanent characteristics of the Church of the apostles. Anglicans hold that the full visible unity of the Church includes the historic episcopal succession.

> Lutherans and Reformed Church members also believe that their ministries stand in apostolic succession. In their ordination rites they emphasize the continuity of the church and its ministry. They can recognize in the historic episcopal succession a sign of the apostolicity of the church. They do not, however, consider it a necessary condition for the full visible unity of the church.

> Nevertheless, we all agree that the use of the sign of the historic episcopal succession does not by itself guarantee the fidelity of a church to every aspect of the apostolic faith, life and mission. Anglicans increasingly recognize that a continuity in apostolic faith, worship and mission has been preserved in churches which have not retained the historic episcopal succession.

> However, Anglicans commend the use of the sign to signify, first, God's promise to be with the church; second, God's call to fidelity and to unity; and third, a commission to realize more fully the permanent characteristics of the church of the apostles.[25]

The key move here from the Anglican side is the combination of a commendation of the use of the sign of apostolicity that the historic episcopate gives with an acknowledgement of non-episcopal ministries in which an apostolic succession of ministry has been maintained in a different form. This position is of course open to criticism from a more traditional catholic perspective in the Church of England on the grounds that it concedes too much to non-episcopal ministries. On the other hand, it is consistent with the position taken up by the Anglican Reformers in the sixteenth century. It is also consistent with the wider ecumenical convergence on the matter reflected in the 1982 World Council of Churches statement, *Baptism, Eucharist and Ministry*, which declares that

> In churches which practise the succession through the episcopate, it is increasingly recognized that a continuity in apostolic faith, worship and mission has been preserved in churches which have not retained the form of the historic episcopate. This recognition finds additional support in the fact that the reality and function of the episcopal ministry have been preserved in many of these churches, with or without the title 'bishop'. Ordination, for example, is always done in them by persons in whom the Church recognizes the authority to transmit the ministerial commission.[26]

Third, we find that recognition is not seen as an end in itself, but as part of a larger journey towards the visible unity of the churches involved and, eventually, the full visible unity of the Church as a whole. This point is made clear in the chapter of *The Reuilly*

Common Statement entitled 'Growth towards full visible unity'. This chapter begins with an explanation of why visible unity is required:

> In order to be truly itself and to fulfil its mission the Church must be seen to be one. The missionary imperative entails the overcoming of the divisions which have kept our churches apart. As our churches grow into the fullness of Christ, so they will grow together in unity (Ephesians 1).[27]

It then goes on to describe what visible unity must include:

> A common proclamation and hearing of the gospel, a common confession of the apostolic faith in word and action.
>
> The sharing of one baptism, the celebrating of one Eucharist and the service of a common ministry (including the exercise of ministry of oversight, episkope).
>
> Bonds of communion which enable the Church at every level to guard and interpret the apostolic faith, to take decisions, to teach authoritatively, to share goods and to bear effective witness in the world. The bonds of communion will possess personal, collegial and communal aspects.[28]

Finally, the chapter declares that from the perspective of the Church of England the commitment to move towards the goal of the full visible unity of the Church means that mutual recognition has to be followed by a further stage:

> Anglicans, on the other hand, make a distinction between the recognition (acknowledgement) of the Church of Christ in another tradition, including the authentic word, sacraments and ministries of the other churches, and a further stage – the formation of a reconciled, common ministry in the historic episcopal succession, together with the establishment of forms of collegial and conciliar oversight. Anglicans speak of this further stage as 'the reconciliation of churches and ministries'.[29]

This reconciliation of churches and ministries within a united, episcopally led church is not seen by the Church of England as being in itself full visible unity. Full visible unity is ultimately an eschatological concept. It is a conversion to Christ and to each other which is a result of the 'work of the Holy Spirit, who opens us up to a life beyond what we can imagine or construct'.[30] Nor should the formation of such a church be seen as simply involving other churches becoming part of the Church of England. What is envisaged is a new form of episcopally led church that would ultimately involve both the Roman Catholic and Orthodox traditions.

What is clear, however, is that for the Church of England the establishment of one organically united, episcopally led church is a key part of the ecumenical process towards which mutual ecclesial recognition has been seen as a stepping-stone.

how recognition has come about

The Church of England has no fixed model for the development of its relationships with other churches. Each relationship has developed in ways that are appropriate in the case of the particular church or churches involved. However, it is possible to see a broad pattern in the way these relationships have developed. First, mutual recognition, for which the favoured term has been mutual 'acknowledgement',[31] has never marked the beginning of such relationships. In every case, mutual acknowledgement has been the fruit of an existing relationship of long standing. In the case of the French Lutheran and Reformed Churches, for example, the relationship can be traced as far back as the sixteenth and seventeenth centuries.[32] What mutual acknowledgement does is to give formal expression to these existing relationships and commit the churches involved to continuing to grow together and work together in the future. Second, acknowledgement has always been between the Church of England and an equivalent body. Individual Church of England parish churches have developed relationships with local churches from other traditions, but because in the Church of England theological and ecclesiological matters are decided at a national level, this is the level at which formal recognition of other churches has had to take place. Third, when the context has made this appropriate, acknowledgement has taken place as a result of a multilateral dialogue involving the other British and Irish Anglican Churches. This was true of the Reuilly agreement and was also true, for example, of the Porvoo agreement with the Nordic and Baltic Lutheran Churches. Fourth, acknowledgement has taken place as a result of what are known as 'formal conversations'.

'Informal' conversations, such as those which provide the context for this chapter, are authorized by the Church of England's Council for Christian Unity and are really a 'testing of the waters' or 'getting to know you' exercise in which both sides in the conversation seek to discover where they have currently got to in their mutual relationship. The Anglicans in such informal conversations do not have the remit to draw up an ecumenical agreement to bring about acknowledgement of another church or set of churches. Should a series of informal conversations indicate that the circumstances were right for a formal agreement to be explored, the Council for Christian Unity would then need to seek authorization from General Synod for the Church of England to enter into 'formal' conversations with this end in view.

Thus in the Anglican–Methodist context, the informal conversations between Anglicans and Methodists produced the document *Commitment to Mission and Unity* which recommended that matters should be taken further and this recommendation then led to the establishment by General Synod and the Methodist Conference of the formal conversations that produced *An Anglican–Methodist Covenant*.

looking to the future

As has been explained previously, formal mutual acknowledgement is a way of enhancing an existing relationship between churches and committing them to continue to grow and work together in future. If the relationship between the Church of England and the churches of the Baptist Union of Great Britain continues to grow in the ways described elsewhere in this report, those bodies may reach the stage at which it is felt right to explore the possibility of putting the relationship on a more formal basis.

The Baptist Union of Great Britain is already listed as one of the bodies with whom the Church of England has ecumenical relations and can enter into Local Ecumenical Partnerships under the terms of Canons B 43 and B 44 of the Church of England's Code of Canon Law. This listing has taken place under the provisions of the 1988 Ecumenical Relations Measure on the grounds that the churches of the Baptist Union of Great Britain are churches that subscribe to the doctrine of the Holy Trinity and administer the sacraments of baptism and Holy Communion.[33] This listing is significant because it means that the Church of England already gives Baptist churches a degree of implicit acknowledgement as 'apostolic' churches. The existence of this degree of implicit acknowledgement arguably indicates that formal acknowledgement would not in principle be impossible if it were felt to be appropriate at some point in the future.

The precise form that a process of mutual acknowledgement might take is something that cannot be predicted at this stage. For the reasons noted above there would have to be some form of national agreement between the Church of England and the Baptist Union of Great Britain, and the principle of ecumenical consistency means that what was agreed would have to be congruent with the other ecumenical agreements that the Church of England has entered into. These two constraints apart, the fact that the Church of England has no set model for the development of its relationships with other churches means that it would be free to develop a process of formal acknowledgement that would reflect the specific nature of its relationship with the Baptist Union of Great Britain at the time when acknowledgement took place.

One final point that needs to be noted, however, is that if the relationship between the Baptist Union of Great Britain and the Church of England is to continue to grow, there are four important issues which were not tackled in these informal conversations, that would need to be tackled at some point in the future.

1   The first of these is the issue of the goal of the ecumenical process. As has been explained, the Church of England sees the establishment of one organically united, episcopally led church as a key part of the ecumenical process. What would need to be explored is how this part of the Church of England's ecumenical vision relates to the way(s) in which Baptists view the future development of ecumenism, and how Anglicans and Baptists would be able to continue to develop a closer relationship even if there is a difference between their respective theologies in this area.

2   The second is the issue of confessing the apostolic faith together. The Church of England is a church that gives expression to its faith through the recitation of the catholic creeds, and its ecumenical agreements have included relatively detailed statements of what the churches involved

agree on in matters of faith. Baptists, on the other hand, do not regularly recite the catholic creeds as part of their worship, and although they have produced statements of faith in the past, more recently Baptists have not seen detailed agreement in faith as a necessary condition for the development of relationships between churches. As before, this is an area in which Baptists and Anglicans would need to explore how their different approaches relate to each other and their significance for the further development of the relationship between the Church of England and the Baptist Union of Great Britain.

3   The third issue is that of eucharistic theology. As we have noted, agreement in faith about the Eucharist has been a feature of previous Church of England ecumenical agreements, and if the Church of England and the Baptist Union of Great Britain were to grow closer together the question of their respective understandings of the Eucharist or the Lord's Supper would also need to be explored. This is because, as Roman Catholic theologians have rightly reminded us, if Christians are to participate in the Eucharist together with integrity, there needs to be not only a shared willingness to participate in the eucharistic liturgy, but also a shared understanding of what the sacrament means.

4   Finally, the whole area of what ministry and priesthood belongs to the Church of Christ would need to be explored further. While our report has considered various aspects of the related questions of apostolicity and oversight, we have not been able to undertake the sort of thorough study of ministry and ordination and its relation to the royal priesthood that would be required for the step of formal ecclesial acknowledgement to become possible for the Church of England.

chapter eight

apostolicity and recognition: a Baptist contribution

introduction: learning to see each other as true churches

The stories we have told of historical cooperation and current local ecumenical relationships between Anglicans and Baptists imply that some level of implicit recognition is already going on, and indeed is quite common. From a Baptist perspective, this local implicit recognition is theologically significant. This paper is an attempt to describe why that is the case by making the implicit theology of Baptist practice explicit, and so offer some suggestions as to how what is an informal and patchy 'seeing of each other' as apostolic churches might be placed on a firmer theological foundation. First, though, one more story, which is a composite fiction. Each element in the story below is or has been true of a particular local situation; pulling them together describes the levels to which implicit recognition of Anglicans by Baptists might currently reach, and so poses the question in its sharpest form.

> Great Pagford is a small market town in the home counties, home to St Peter's (Church of England), St Michael's (Roman Catholic), Great Pagford Baptist Chapel, and Central Methodist Church. During the 1970s, friendship between the local clergy led to inter-church cooperation, first on social justice events (Christian Aid Week and so on), and then some sharing of services, beginning during the Week of Prayer for Christian Unity. In 1979 the churches were moved to draw up and sign an ecumenical covenant, affirming their friendship and partnership in the gospel, and committing themselves to work together where they could in the future.

> The covenant became an established part of local church life, and various forms of cooperation developed. The churches eagerly embraced the concept of ecumenical house groups during Lent, and 'pulpit exchanges' became a regular feature

of their life. Together, they started a midweek lunchtime 'shoppers' service', held in the Methodist church (because of where it was), but run by each of the churches in turn. Personal friendships led to further inter-church cooperation, and when (for instance) St Michael's ran a school of prayer led by nuns from a nearby convent, it was natural to open the invitation to members of the other churches. The tenth anniversary of the covenant in 1989 was celebrated with a week of events, culminating in a service to reaffirm the covenant. After some discussion, the churches sought permission from the appropriate authorities to celebrate a joint Eucharist at this service. This was refused (by the Roman Catholic diocese), but even having expressed the desire felt important to the churches. The covenant relationship was also formalized in a local Churches Together group, reflecting advances in national ecumenism.

In the 1990s the covenant was an important part of the life of each of the churches. When priests/ministers left, the churches asked that their replacements be committed to local ecumenism. Joint services became monthly events on Sunday evenings, and several each year were held on Sunday mornings. As they all faced the problems of shrinking children's and youth work, they began to run joint midweek youth clubs, and then joint work on Sunday mornings. Joint 'introducing Christianity' courses, modelled on the Alpha pattern, were introduced. Today, which of the four churches young people and adults join is almost an afterthought, as virtually all those who come into the churches come through a thoroughly ecumenical route. Joint Eucharists are now a regular feature, with whatever combinations of celebrant and church that are permitted by the various denominations being employed.

This is a composite account, but there are local situations where every feature above is currently happening, and not just in the special cases of single- or multi-congregation LEPs. As such, it is an extreme example of the levels to which local ecumenical recognition has risen. In this (fictional) example, the Baptist church appears simply to recognize the others: in Baptist understanding it is possessed of the fullness of the one Church of Jesus Christ in its own right, without need for any wider structure, and so its decision to share its worship and mission without reserve is decisive. In a sense, the challenge for ecumenical work from the Baptist side is to make as much theological sense of this recognition as possible, and also to point out where, if anywhere, the decisions of this Baptist church failed to be true to generally accepted Baptist positions. This paper must thus start from the acknowledgement that, in certain local contexts, some Baptist churches have already recognized some Church of England parishes virtually without qualification, although in other cases the attitude is much more reserved. The theological questions are: how this actual recognition may be understood; whether the theology implied by the decisions and actions of a local church is adequate and coherent; and whether such examples of local recognition can imply anything about overall relationships between the Baptist Union of Great Britain and the Church of England. We already think, without formal recognition, that we can see the one Church of Jesus Christ in each other's churches. How can we put this affirmation on a firmer theological foundation, and what might be its implications for our life together?

a Baptist view

For the final piece of preamble, the subtitle needs stressing: this is *a* Baptist contribution, i.e. one among several Baptist views that are possible, although agreed by all the Baptist participants in these conversations. No doubt this theme, that the Baptist Union of Great Britain does not have the power (or, indeed, the desire) to generate agreement amongst its churches on issues that seem central and non-negotiable to our Anglican sisters and brothers, is in danger of becoming both tedious and irritating, especially as it impacts on our desire to move forward, but we cannot pretend that it is otherwise. Particularly when issues of recognition are at stake, this is important: it is conceivable that a situation might be reached at some point in the future where the Baptist Union of Great Britain institutionally recognizes certain ministries or practices through its Council and resolution of Assembly, and commends such recognition to its member churches. In such a situation, however, a particular local Baptist church would not and could not be compelled to acquiesce. Some churches, no doubt, would sever their ties with the Union in protest, but others would remain within whilst refusing to agree. (This, indeed, is currently the situation with the ordination of women to the ministry in our churches; for most of the last century this has been supported nationally, and is presently promoted at various levels, but some churches within the Union would still not open their pulpit to a woman.)

an issue of ecclesiology

These reflections are perhaps a helpful way into the substance of this paper. At the heart of the questions at stake is an issue of ecclesiology: Baptists, of course, confess their belief in one Church, holy, catholic and apostolic, and pray and work and long for the eschatological day when that one Church will be fully revealed. Before that final ingathering, however, Baptists see the one Church of Christ as most clearly visible in the gathered, covenanted congregation of believers, from which ministry and trans-local structures emerge. Hence, and again risking tedium, the Baptist Union of Great Britain is not a church, but a fellowship of churches, covenanted to know the mind of Christ together, for the furtherance of the gospel and mutual support. All who are willing to acknowledge certain minimal points of agreement (enshrined in the Baptist Union of Great Britain Declaration of Principle, Appendix 2) will be welcomed into this covenant fellowship.

Most churches within this fellowship would currently understand apostolicity as having two significant components: first, and in a fairly straightforwardly Reformed way, a church is apostolic if it maintains and teaches the apostolic faith, and maintains and practises the apostolic worship, particularly the act of preaching and the two dominical sacraments of baptism and Eucharist; second, a church is apostolic if it participates in the apostolic mission, if it continues to hear and obey the basic apostolic commission to go and make disciples in Jerusalem and to the ends of the earth (Matthew 28; Acts 1). The order here is not one of priority, but of logic: to the extent that making disciples involves teaching the faith, and their participation in worship, the teaching is logically prior to the mission. Historically, it has also been a common Baptist position to insist that true apostolicity demands a certain church order. This has two parts: first, it has been asserted that the presence of certain officers – a pastor, deacons, and (perhaps) elders – is demanded by the apostolic teaching, and so belongs to apostolicity. These officers minister the sacraments to the people (traditionally, the most visible role of Baptist deacons has been to serve the eucharistic elements to the people), and maintain the teaching ministry; they also take the lead in the apostolic mission. Secondly, and more importantly, congregational church government has been seen as vital: only if the ultimate decision-making body in the church is the Church Meeting can a church claim to be governed by Christ, and the involvement of other ecclesiastical or political authorities has been seen as interfering with his rule. Church discipline, often mooted by Reformed traditions as an extra mark of the Church, is important in Baptist understanding, and is to be exercised by the Church Meeting, where, for Baptists, the rule of Christ is discerned.

Today, Baptists will generally share the developing consensus that it is not quite as easy as it used to be thought to discern particular normative patterns of church leadership in the New Testament, and so there is some variety in Baptist life, which is not seen as an impediment to apostolicity. Whilst the rhetoric around church government is less inflammatory, however, a church desiring to join the Baptist Union of Great Britain will still be required to have a Church Meeting that cannot be over-ruled by any human authority. Historically (in the common cause made by the three denominations of 'Old Dissent') and presently (through LEPs and other formal and informal ecumenical relationships), however, Baptists have been ready either formally to recognize, or to act as if they recognize, the presence of the one Church of Christ in churches governed in other ways. Certainly, the discussions elsewhere in this report of episcopacy as currently practised by Anglicans demonstrate that the old polemical points about dictatorial rule are no longer even remotely true, if they ever were; and whilst Baptists will continue to want to insist that there is something proper about the practice of the Church Meeting, this insistence need not deny the possibility of affirming that Christ can speak and rule through Parochial Church Councils and Synods, where these structures humbly and prayerfully seek to be obedient to him.

As a denomination Baptists increasingly see mission as central to what it is to be church, and so would resist any suggestion that apostolicity is first about keeping and celebrating the deposit of faith, or about patterns of order, and only subsequently about transmitting it. Indeed, Baptists would feel that the apostolic teaching has simply not been heard, and the mind of Christ not properly discerned in Church Meeting, if the mission imperative is not held to be absolutely central. The sacraments might also be seen by many Baptists as missionary events: understanding worship as a participation in the mission of the triune God, Baptists would suggest that central amongst the various meanings of baptism is an act of ordination to the apostolic mission, and of witness to the saving power of Christ; more speculatively, within the mystery of the institution of the Eucharist, the Pauline assertion that 'as often as you eat the bread and drink the cup, you proclaim the Lord's death, until he comes' might be seen by Baptists as an opportunity to develop a eucharistic missiology.

apostolic succession

The language of 'apostolic succession' is unfamiliar to Baptists, as is the requirement for traceable historical continuity which the phrase is sometimes used to mean. A group of (baptized) Christian believers who make covenant together to worship, learn from the Word, seek Christ's will and mutual accountability in meeting together, and spread the good news of Christ are, just so, 'church', with no qualifications necessary. Baptist thought would go on to suggest that they may – indeed, should – call one or more of their number to exercise the ministry of word and sacrament amongst them, recognizing the prior call of Christ. Nevertheless, it has been a persistent theme within Baptist ecclesiology that Christian churches belong together, not apart (the doctrine of associating), and so expressions of trans-local ecclesial life constantly appear. These are not merely utilitarian: the churches of the Baptist Union of Great Britain covenant together not just because they gain much by so doing, but because they believe that they should make covenant: Christ has one rule and one body, and so those who can recognize each other as walking according to Christ's rule and being members of his body cannot refuse each other covenant fellowship. At its strongest, this ethical demand has been described as analogous to the requirement that Christians belong to a church, and so it is a legitimate derivation from a strand of Baptist ecclesiology to describe membership of wider structures in sacramental terms: just as belonging to a local church is both a demand of the gospel and a great means of grace for the Christian believer, so joining in wider fellowship is both a demand upon churches and a way God chooses to bless them.

This is how the ethical demand implied in the identification of catholicity as a mark of the Church might be understood within Baptist ecclesiology. Christian churches belong together, not apart, and so some level of formal recognition of other apostolic churches is a necessary part of being church authentically. Baptists would want to understand this, not in terms of some sort of incompleteness of the local church, considered in itself: the

Eucharist and mission of a particular congregation need nothing more to make them valid. Instead, Baptists would think of this demand as a duty incumbent on each particular local church to make and maintain appropriate covenant relationship with all other fellowships that are recognized as holding to the apostolic faith; a refusal so to do would suggest a failure to follow the rule of Christ, and so would indeed be an ecclesiological failure. Thus for Baptists the local congregation is the basic instantiation of church, this side of the Eschaton, whereas other traditions tend to look to the diocese. The early Baptist practice of calling local ministers bishops points to this shift in understanding, and also indicates a belief that *episkopos* and *presbuteros* refer to the same order of ministry in the New Testament.

This alternative account of the ministry of oversight is important to understanding how Baptist ecclesiology can relate to emerging ecumenical convergences. Baptists would see their view as maintaining theologically important links between *episkope*/oversight, sacramental presidency, the teaching ministry and church fellowship. That is, the ecumenically significant ideas that the bishop is the primary eucharistic minister and the one who preserves and transmits the apostolic faith would be understood by Baptists to imply that the 'bishop' (i.e. local minister) is the one who normally celebrates the Eucharist, and teaches the faithful. The 'ministry of Word and sacrament' exercised in the local congregation is precisely and straightforwardly episcopal, in Baptist understanding. Indeed, where Baptist churches share a minister, the usual pattern is just what is suggested by that phrase: it is not that a church with multiple congregations is formed; it is rather that one person exercises a ministry of oversight in two different places. Baptists would want to note that their practice here is consonant with the practice of *episkope* in the immediate sub-apostolic period, and so not an innovation within the Christian tradition.

Having said all this, the ordained ministry has become a particular focus for wider fellowship in Baptist life. In practice, it has often or always been the case that churches seeking to call pastors, or struggling in their relationships with their pastors, find particular help and support from outside, whether formalized through the Baptist Union of Great Britain structures, or through much more informal contact. Whilst fellowship between churches always has as one of its elements the desire to know better the mind of Christ, experience suggests that it is particularly in regard to questions of ministry that this becomes pressing. The practice of asking (ordained) representatives of the wider family of churches to be involved in ordination and induction services, often expressed in early Baptist life by the phrase 'ordination of elders by elders', has been an important expression of the belonging together of churches in Baptist life, and would now generally be considered a matter of good order within the Baptist family of churches, with a regional minister ideally taking the lead role. There is in this, however, no sense of the development of a wider order of ministry: regional ministers have no further ordination/consecration that sets them apart from their fellow ministers; their particular function of representing the wider family of Baptist churches makes their presidency of other ordinations particularly appropriate, but no more than this.

Modern Baptists would probably resist any attempt to describe these links between churches as part of the 'apostolicity' of the churches (they might find it easier to acknowledge they are part of our catholicity, as these links point towards the unity of the one Church of Christ). There have been, however, suggestions of apostolic language at times in British Baptist life: the early General Baptists, for example, expressed their trans-local unity through the appointment of 'Messengers', a word which carried clear apostolic overtones. Given that at the key moments of ordination and induction there is an involvement of the wider family of churches, and so an explicit or implicit acknowledgement that this ordination is to the ministry of the universal Church, not just of this local fellowship, it might be that some of the substance of what is demanded in language of 'apostolic succession' could be seen as present amongst us, even if we resist the term. If Baptists had to use the term 'apostolic succession', they would probably choose to see it in terms of the handing on (traditioning) and the subsequent continuity of the various aspects of apostolicity identified above. The apostolic faith, worship, order and mission are handed on to successive generations in various ways: through ordination; through the teaching ministry; through the baptism and reception of new church members; and even through the eucharistic celebration. This last becomes clear when we consider the distinctive form of Baptist eucharistic liturgy, in which the words of institution are spoken not to God, in eucharistic prayer, but to the congregation, in telling and so perpetuating the gospel story (a particularly Baptist form of the more general Christian practice of transmitting teaching through worship, classically expressed in Prosper of Aquitaine's famous slogan *lex orandi lex credendi)*. In all these ways there is a preservation and continuation of the apostolic mission, and so (in Baptist terms) a true apostolic succession.

discerning apostolicity

In attempting to discern apostolicity within the Church of England, then, Baptists would ask the Reformation question 'Is the Word of God rightly preached, and are the sacraments rightly celebrated?' and they would also look for a continuing commitment to the apostolic mission, and a willingness to walk according to the rule of Christ. Temperamentally and theologically they would want to ask the question of each particular congregation, not of the Church of England as a whole: temperamentally in that Baptists have (often over the last two centuries or so, and occasionally before that – see Chapter 1) tended to be prepared to work and worship with particular Church of England parish churches on the evidence of their life and witness, even whilst maintaining a heavy rhetoric against Anglicanism as a monolithic entity; theologically because Baptist belief that each local church is entire and complete would seem to force them to ask this question at this level.

This said, however, Baptist trans-local bodies are prepared to associate together as fellowships of churches. Thus a particular local church relates to the Fellowship of British Baptists, the European Baptist Federation, and the Baptist World Alliance not directly, but because it is a member church of the Baptist Union of Great Britain and the Baptist Union of Great Britain belongs to each of these bodies. There is no explicit theological justification of this practice, but one is easily constructed: if two trans-local ecclesial bodies (e.g. the Baptist Union of Great Britain and the Baptist Union of Scotland) each demand that the conditions for apostolicity are being met before admitting any church into their respective memberships, then they can enter into covenant fellowship together on behalf of their member churches because the demands that their member churches would make before entering into fellowship appear to be fulfilled. On this basis, there can be a presumption that each particular church teaches the apostolic faith, and celebrates the apostolic worship, and walks according to the rule of Christ, and so that covenant relationship is possible (indeed, necessary). Baptist churches, that is to say, are able to consider each other as apostolic through an attitude of charity and trust. This was the procedure followed when the Baptist Union of Great Britain joined Churches Together in England, and it might also suggest a way in which Baptists could affirm the apostolicity of the Church of England as a body.

associating and covenanting with other churches

The issue remaining is whether the Baptist ecclesial imperative to make covenant fellowship with other churches which we recognize as apostolic can be applied to the Church of England. Thus, the doctrine of associating demands further discussion here. Baptist churches associate with each other because they believe they should: they belong together, not apart. They associate for the purposes of knowing the mind of Christ, mission, and mutual support. Associating has always been seen as a serious matter (even when major disagreements affect the Union, it is noticeable that it is a small minority of those churches who disagree with the majority line that choose to disassociate themselves and resign their Union membership). Baptists are increasingly recovering their historical language of 'covenant' to name what goes on, which stresses the seriousness of the matter further: covenants may occasionally be dissolved by mutual agreement, but cannot sensibly be unilaterally withdrawn from. Further, covenant language makes clear what has always been held: that associating is a theological reality, one that involves God's evangelical call to God's people and faithful human response.

The patterns of associating for Baptist churches have always been flexible: different formal structures currently exist at regional, national, continental and global levels. Informal (but nonetheless real) structures of associating are also common: these may be more local (a cluster of churches in a particular town, for example); trans-local but related to a particular missiological context or theological position (groups of rural churches working together at county or national level; churches influenced by charismatic renewal supporting each other); or involving other patterns (church twinning relationships would be understood as an expression of associating, for instance). Associating may also exist across denominational boundaries, and always has, as can be seen from various examples: historical structures representing the 'Three Denominations', dating back to the seventeenth century;

evangelical structures dating mainly from the nineteenth century; and twentieth-century ecumenical structures. The most recent Baptist Union of Great Britain discussions on associating, which introduced the language of clusters, explicitly acknowledged, and indeed encouraged, the possibility of ecumenical clustering as an appropriate way for Baptist churches to express their desire and need to associate. It would be true to say that some of our churches would see their primary associating as ecumenical, being more closely bound into (for example) the Evangelical Alliance or a local ecumenical structure than they are into Baptist life.

It is clear from such recognitions that associating is not an all-or-nothing matter: churches can covenant together seriously at various different levels of commitment, and each of these would be a valid expression of associating. If, however, associating demands a recognition of apostolicity, as it must, it is appropriate to ask how such various and wide associating can happen. Baptist life is not so ordered that such questions are asked and debated before the practices of associating that give rise to them are engaged in, but some theological justification is available. After all, these are not just questions for ecumenical relationships from a Baptist perspective. Sharp disagreements over certain matters of biblical interpretation, church order, missionary activities, or sacramental liturgical practice are hardly unknown within Baptist life.

Obviously, the conditions for apostolicity outlined above are not simple yes/no matters. In no church is the preaching of the Word 'pure' in the sense that it could not be improved or bettered, nor is there anywhere a perfect celebration of the Eucharist. The confession that, despite our best efforts, we have not walked according to Christ's rule is a standard part of the Sunday worship of most or all Baptist churches; churches do constantly re-evaluate their structures in a desire to be more faithful to Christ; and no church would claim that it was perfectly fulfilling the apostolic missionary mandate. Given all this, if these are the marks of apostolicity, then apostolicity would seem to be an aspiration, an ideal that is striven towards but not reached. Historically, this might be expressed by the standard Reformed confession of the provisionality of all ecclesial judgements (*ecclesia reformata semper reformanda*), which has been particularly prominent in Baptist life, with the conviction that 'the Lord hath yet more light and truth to break forth from his word' being prominent in history as well as hymnody; in the eighteenth century Baptist discussions of even such a central tenet as the proper subjects of baptism regularly acknowledged the possibility that a greater grasp of the truth might demonstrate the Baptist position to be wrong.

This sense of apostolicity as an aspiration is probably the general Baptist understanding, but it stands in need of some further theological development. Credally, it is necessary to confess that the Church is apostolic, not merely striving to be so, and this suggests that apostolicity should be understood as an eschatological reality, rather than an aspirational one, just as the unity and holiness of the Church are eschatologically and so proleptically real. The right preaching of the Word finds its eschatological fulfilment in the saints' eternal work of repeating the glories of the gospel story to the Father in worship. The Eucharist is transformed and fulfilled in the Messianic feast, where Christ will take his place as host at the meal, and so the yearning and longing and remembering and hoping that so mark the present celebration of the communion meal will all be fully met. Baptism is fulfilled when the Spirit is finally given to the Church without measure. One day, we shall know fully, even as we are fully known. One day, God's mission will embrace all creation. Therefore any church's apostolicity consists in its anticipation of the coming kingdom, just as its holiness does.

Given this, a Baptist church asking whether it is able to recognize another church as apostolic is not asking that the doctrine and worship of that church be perfect, but that they be on the way to being eschatologically perfected. Once again, the historic analogy with church membership is appropriate: in receiving a person into membership, a Baptist church will investigate his or her faith and character, but there is no demand for perfection, merely a desire to discern that this is someone whose understanding of what it means to walk according to the gospel of Christ is close enough to that of the fellowship that they may walk together, and who shows evidence of a desire, in humble dependence on the Spirit, to walk that way. A church asking whether it can recognize apostolicity in another fellowship is looking for very similar things: some degree of shared understanding of the promises and demands of the gospel, and some evidence of a serious desire to live according to those promises, and to fulfil those demands.

'Some evidence', and other such qualifications, are obviously somewhat slippery matters. There have always been, and still are,

Baptists who set the standards high; confident of their own ability to discern the truth of the gospel, they judge others according to their lights and find many or most wanting, and so refuse to engage in ecumenical pursuits on a local or national level. More typically, however, Baptists have been less certain of their own judgements, taking seriously the Reformation slogan that an *ecclesia reformata* must be *semper reformanda*. Baptist confessions are classically marked by such phrases as 'unless and until the Spirit shall give us more light . . .', and so are more charitable in their assessment of others. Historically, British Baptist ecumenism was largely restricted to other Free Churches, but there was significant doctrinal latitude (when many Free Churches drifted into Arianism, Socinianism, and then Unitarianism, there was debate amongst Baptists as to whether this removed them from the bounds of fellowship), and common cause could be made with Presbyterians who did not share the crucial Baptist practice of Church Meeting. Shared evangelical beliefs in the latter half of the eighteenth century, and the repeal of much of the discriminatory legislation contained in the Clarendon Code in 1828, extended Baptists' ecumenical welcome to some, at least, of the Established Church, although this welcome was based on doctrinal agreement within evangelicalism. Into the latter half of the twentieth century, it was extended further to Roman Catholics and others, and now it would seem that most churches within the Baptist Union of Great Britain would have little difficulty in affirming any member church of the World Council of Churches as in some sense apostolic.

questions of baptism and church order

The question must remain, however, whether in such recognition there is an abandonment, rather than an application, of traditional principles of Baptist ecclesiology. In particular, questions of baptism and church order loom large. Is it the case that Baptists can find the theological resources to explain their lived recognition of Anglican (and other) churches? Three lines of argument suggest that they might.

First, given the eschatological arguments developed here, the assumption cannot be that Baptist polity is simply right, and a standard by which all other polities can be measured. Instead, every Christian church is pursuing (in the old Reformed language) a theology on the way, advancing its best current understanding of the faith, but acknowledging that such understandings are always provisional and subject to future correction. Realizing this should not lessen conviction, but rather increase humility and the willingness to recognize those who differ, even on dearly held beliefs, as fellow-pilgrims.

Secondly, other arguments might be developed from the history of British Baptist thought. As already indicated, some Baptists (including John Bunyan, Daniel Turner and Robert Robinson) have offered an exposition of Romans 14–15 which – whatever its exegetical validity – allows a necessary theological point to be made, and develops standard themes of Baptist theology (see pages 39–40). Building on classical Baptist ideas of freedom of belief, they read the text to suggest that it is improper for Christians to judge each other on such matters; rather they should leave judgement to Christ, who knows and accepts his own. The argument is slightly question begging, of course, in that the question of who counts as a Christian is rather the point to be proved, but it suggests an attempt, and a theologically serious one, to address the root issue. It might be that a development of this approach would allow a more generous estimation of the baptismal polity of the Church of England than Baptists have traditionally followed.

Finally, within this report an account of Christian initiation as a composite process is developed which serves not to remove, but to relativize the differences between Baptist and Anglican practices. We might continue to disagree on the proper ordering of the various moments of the process, but if we can recognize that a very similar process is being followed, in which baptism plays a crucial part, then we might see the differing polities as less straightforwardly opposed than has sometimes been the case, and in fact creating an openness to the sort of recognition described in the previous section.

There are, then, theological arguments available to suggest that Baptists have, at least at times, been able to extend the recognition that has been described without abandoning their ecclesiological principles.

evidence for apostolicity

The evidence that leads Baptist churches to regard other churches (including other Baptist churches) as eschatologically, and so genuinely, apostolic may come in many forms. At the local level, it will probably involve a judgement of the life and witness of a particular fellowship – 'by their fruits shall you know them'. Between Baptist churches in membership of different trans-local fellowships (e.g. the Baptist Union of Great Britain and the Baptist Union of Scotland), it is based on an attitude of charity and trust. In this report arguments have been developed about sacramental theology which, it is hoped, gives Baptists reason to believe that Anglican churches, and the Church of England as a body, can be regarded in the same way.

Mainstream British Baptist practice (certainly the practice of the Baptist Union of Great Britain and the majority of its member churches) suggests that all that is demanded before some measure of associating is possible is a commitment to a certain level of theological orthodoxy on central questions (e.g. the Trinity, Christology and salvation through Christ – those matters contained, for instance, in the standard Churches Together agreement), those principles being worked out in practice, a shared commitment to mission, and some willingness for reciprocal recognition. To note one specific example, Baptists do in fact associate with Salvationists, and so there is no question of differences in sacramental theology, or in understandings of how Christ may speak through the structures of a church, being sufficient to prevent some measure of associating. The stronger bonds of associating, involving the inclusion of deeper mutual commitments in the covenant relationship, will naturally grow from the perceived closeness of the associating churches, but that 'closeness' might involve theological, geographical, missiological or many other factors. Clearly, for certain specific forms of relationship to obtain, certain conditions must be met (sacramental life will not be shared without some mutual recognition of ministry and sacrament, for instance), but forms of associating are variable, and so these are merely specific barriers to specific relationships. (It would, for example, be conceivable, although extreme, for a Baptist church to share premises, finances, youth work, mission and a considerable amount of its worship with another congregation with whom it could not share a sacramental life.) Baptist churches can – and many do – recognize Church of England parish churches as in some sense apostolic, even whilst sharply disagreeing with certain elements of Anglican practice, because apostolicity is an eschatological reality in which they can recognize Anglican churches' participation.

theology of ecumenical involvement

The final stage of the argument is fairly obvious: in Baptist ecclesiology, the theology of involvement in ecumenical structures is precisely the same as the theology of involvement in denominational structures. A Baptist church participating fully in a Churches Together group with the local parish church (for example) relates to that parish church on exactly the same terms as it relates to other Baptist churches within its local region, assuming the Churches Together group is built on a covenantal basis. At present, many Baptist churches are according recognition to Church of England parish churches with which they participate in various different ways – and this has been the case, although more rarely, for many decades (there are records of joint eucharistic services in 1845, to celebrate the founding of the Evangelical Alliance). The extent, the depth, of the associating varies, and so the level of recognition varies too, but this chapter has indicated that this is as true between Baptist churches themselves as it is between Baptist and other churches.

mutual recognition? summary and questions to the churches

Apostolicity is an essential mark of the one Church of Jesus Christ. It is demonstrated:

- *by maintenance and faithful transmission of the apostolic doctrine ('the pure preaching of the Word');*

- *by proper celebration of the dominical sacraments of baptism and Eucharist ('the due ministration of the sacraments');*

- *by some form of historical continuity, or at least some intention to stand in continuity, with the church of the apostles;*

- *and by participation in the apostolic mission.*

Neither of our communions has seen the apostolicity of other bodies as a simple yes-or-no question. The Church of England has developed a broadly three-stage process, beginning with implicit recognition ('seeing') of another body as apostolic, proceeding to a formal declaration of that recognition, and thence to a full interchangeability of ministries. The Baptist Union of Great Britain and its churches tend to see less of a distinction between the first two of these stages.

These various stages of recognition could take place at various levels: between local congregations; at an intermediate/diocesan level; nationally; or internationally. For Baptists, the first of these levels (the local) will be decisive, whereas Anglicans will make their authoritative decisions at the third (nationally).

Since we have been able to find a convergence on what it means to be apostolic, we believe that our differing ways of discerning apostolicity should not prevent us from seeing it in each other. We rejoice in the many implicit and informal ways in which Anglicans and Baptists are beginning to recognize each other's apostolicity: through mutual participation in ecumenical instruments and covenants at local, regional, national and international levels; through the inclusion of the Baptist Union of Great Britain in the list of those recognized under the Ecumenical Relations Measure of the Church of England; and through lived fellowship in the gospel in LEPs and other local arrangements. We acknowledge, however, that barriers remain to full mutual recognition. We thus ask the following questions of each other:

1   How much do Baptists and Anglicans share a concern that the life and mission of the Church should stand in continuity with the Church of the Apostles? In particular, can Baptists understand why Anglicans value the ministry of bishops as a sign of historical continuity between the Church of the Apostles and the life and mission of the Church today?

2   How far are Baptists and Anglicans able to see each other's churches as truly sharing in the apostolic mission of the people of God? What might be the consequences for the way that evangelism and church-planting are carried out when Baptists and Anglicans see each other as sharing in that mission? When Baptists affirm the apostolicity of Anglican churches, should they also give some place, within the missionary purposes of God, to the baptism of infants within those churches? If there is an inconsistency here, how could it be resolved?

3   How far can Anglicans and Baptists see the ministries of one another's churches as effective instruments of the Holy Spirit? In particular, can Anglicans see ordained Baptist ministers as exercising a ministry of word and sacrament which is being used by the Holy Spirit to nourish and build up the Church of Christ?

4   Is it possible for Anglicans and Baptists to discern the same reality of pastoral responsibility and oversight (*episkope*) in each other's churches, despite differences in church structures? In particular, can Anglicans discern this oversight in and among Baptist churches, even though there is no bishop according to the Anglican understanding of that office?

5   In the light of these reflections on apostolicity, are Baptists and Anglicans able to see the presence of the one Church of Jesus Christ in each other's churches, and in what ways could this be publicly expressed?

ecumenical context of the conversations

Ecumenical conversations and agreements involving Baptists or the Church of England

multilateral talks

Baptism, Eucharist and Ministry

The first round of Church of England/Baptist Union of Great Britain discussions between 1992 and 2000 reflected on the responses of the two churches to the major multilateral convergence text, *Baptism, Eucharist and Ministry* (1982: BEM). BEM's emphasis on initiation as a process is helpful for both Anglicans and Baptists and is explored in the body of our report. However, the 'Baptism' text does not resolve the issue of 're-baptism' as far as Baptists are concerned. Regarding the 'Eucharist' document, Anglicans and Baptists were agreed that the text does not lay sufficient emphasis on Christ's presence throughout the celebration, although they tend to differ over what is meant by 'effective sign' and 'efficacy'. The 'Ministry' text, with its understanding of the apostolicity of the whole Church and the ministry of oversight, provides Anglicans and Baptists with a context for re-examining together *episkope* – exercised personally, collegially and communally. The group questioned whether there was a sufficient underlying ecclesiology in *Baptism, Eucharist and Ministry* to hold together the catholic and reformed dimensions of the Church.

Called to be One[1]

During the Churches Together in England process *Called to be One*, each meeting of the conversations discussed the provisional responses of the Church of England and the Baptist Union to the questions:

1   How does your church understand the meaning of the word
     Church, and how do you use the word?

2   How does your church understand the meaning of the word
     unity? What kind of unity are you seeking?

3   How does your church understand the meaning of the word
     visible in the phrase *the visible unity of the Church*?

The Baptist Union of Great Britain collated the work for the study
on 'Christian Initiation and Church Membership' and the Church of
England collated the work on 'Ordained Ministry'. The *Called to be
One* process provided an important multilateral background for the
Church of England–Baptist Union of Great Britain informal bilateral.

bilateral talks

International conversations between the Baptist World Alliance and other world communions

The Baptist World Alliance has now completed five international
conversations. The first was with the World Alliance of Reformed
Churches (1973–7), the second with Roman Catholics through the
Vatican Secretariat for Promoting Christian Unity (1984–8), the
third with the Lutheran World Federation (1986–9) and the fourth
with the Mennonite World Conference (1989–92).[2] Significantly,
the conversations with the Lutherans recommended that further
editions of the Lutheran Confessions should contain a statement
indicating that the historic condemnations against Anabaptists 'no
longer apply in our inter-denominational relations', in the context
of the recommendation that 'we mutually recognize each other as
communions within the Church of Christ'.[3] During 1994–7 'pre-
conversations' were held with the Ecumenical Patriarchate of
Constantinople, with the hope that these would continue into
conversations with the Orthodox Church generally, but the Orthodox
representatives withdrew at the end of the initial three-year period.

The fifth set of conversations was between Anglicans and Baptists
worldwide (2000–2005), sponsored by the Baptist World Alliance
and the Anglican Consultative Council.[4] The participants included
local theologians and church leaders in six different regions of the

world, and topics covered were: the importance of continuity, confessing the faith, mission and ministry, baptism and the process of initiation, membership of the Church, the Eucharist (or Lord's Supper), *episkope* (or oversight), and the meaning of recognition. One of the stated aims was 'to look for ways to cooperate in mission and community activities, and to increase our fellowship and common witness to the Gospel'. The report affirmed that Baptists and Anglicans 'share together in the apostolic mission' and can 'see the presence of the church of Jesus Christ in each other's churches'. These conversations happened at the same time as the second stage of the conversations of the Church of England with the Baptist Union of Great Britain, and participants of the British conversations were privileged to be able to monitor the progress of the international ones and draw parallels with them, since two of their members also served on the Continuation Committee of the international conversations. Like the conversations between the Church of England and the Baptist Union of Great Britain, the report of the international Anglican–Baptist conversations ended not with recommendations but with questions and challenges to the churches of both communions.

The Meissen Agreement between the Church of England and the Evangelical Church of Germany (EKD)

In 1988 the report of the Meissen conversations, *On the Way to Visible Unity*, was published.[5] The report first sets out a common understanding of the visible unity of the Church to which the partners are committed. The portrait of visible unity owes much to the three-fold description agreed by the Vancouver Assembly of the World Council of Churches. The full visible unity of Christ's Church must include: a common confession of the apostolic faith in word and life, the sharing of one baptism, the celebration of one Eucharist and the service of a reconciled common ministry, and bonds of communion (structures) which enable the Church to guard and interpret the apostolic faith and to bear effective witness in the world. The report lists ten agreements in faith which the churches already share. Here it harvests the work of international bilateral and multilateral dialogues, rather than repeating the theological work so recently done by the churches. One consequence of the use of international theological documents is that a consistency is maintained with regional developments and with the position of world communions. The report is honest about where difference still remains. Lutheran, Reformed and United Churches in the EKD, though increasingly prepared to appreciate episcopal succession 'as a sign of apostolicity of the life of the whole Church, hold that this particular form of *episkope* should not become a necessary condition for full visible unity'. The Anglican understanding of full visible unity, on the other hand, includes the historic episcopal succession with the full interchangeability of ministers.

On the basis of the agreed portrait of full visible unity, stated agreements in faith, and an honest recognition of the outstanding differences, the churches concerned signed a formal Declaration in 1991 (*The Meissen Agreement*) committing themselves to a closer degree of shared life appropriate to the degree of their agreement in faith and the close friendships which had existed over many years.

In the Declaration the churches first made mutual acknowledgments: an acknowledgment of one another's churches as belonging to the One, Holy, Catholic and Apostolic Church of Jesus Christ and truly participating in the apostolic mission; the acknowledgment of each other as churches in which the Word of God is authentically preached and the sacraments are duly administered; and the acknowledgement of each other's ordained ministries as given by God and as instruments of his grace. For Anglicans the official acknowledgement of the ecclesial authenticity of the ordained ministry of the EKD marks a significant stage on the way to visible unity. It does not, however, bring about the interchangeability of ministries. Beyond the acknowledgement of authentic ministries in other churches lies the bringing together of separated ministries within the bringing together of the life of communities. This greater unity is signified, for Anglicans, in a single ministry in the historic episcopal succession within a single collegial and conciliar life.

Nevertheless, in the formal Declaration the churches make binding commitments to one another. These are commitments to work at the outstanding differences, to establish forms of joint oversight which will maintain the new relationships, to encourage exchange and twinnings, to receive communion in each other's churches and for clergy to share in the celebration of the Eucharist, not in place of one another nor concelebrating, but in such a way that the closeness of the churches is visibly testified to and the churches are beckoned to move towards a single interchangeable ministry and common life and mission.

After synodical approval in the respective churches, the Meissen Declaration was solemnly signed and celebrated in eucharistic services in Westminster Abbey and in Berlin in 1991. It seemed to many that the unity of the Church and the unity of the world were held together in those great services.

The Meissen Commission was set up to give oversight to the developing relation between the partner churches and has been instrumental in holding the churches to the commitments they made. A series of theological conferences has begun to explore the remaining outstanding issue of *episkope* and episcopacy, apostolicity and succession, and their proceedings have been published.[6]

The Porvoo Agreement between the Anglican Churches of Britain and Ireland and the Nordic and Baltic Lutheran Churches[7]

Between 1909 and 1951 theological conversations between Anglicans and Lutherans led to a number of piecemeal agreements between the Church of England and some of the Nordic and Baltic Lutheran Churches. In 1988 it was suggested that the time was now right to look at these several agreements in the light of more recent theological conversations in order to see whether Lutheran and Anglican Churches could move to closer visible unity. In 1989 conversations began, aware that momentous changes were taking place, a *kairos* moment for the unity of the churches in northern Europe. The missionary imperative was a dominant theme throughout the talks.

The Anglican Churches of Britain and Ireland and the Nordic and Baltic Lutheran Churches are all episcopal churches and all now have bishops consecrated in a continuous episcopal succession. However, the first post-Reformation bishops of the churches of Denmark, Norway and Iceland were consecrated by a presbyter.

The report of the conversations published in 1993 follows the same simple logic and dynamic as *The Meissen Common Statement.* Having affirmed the imperative for shared mission in the new European context, brought about by the overthrow of communism, the report sets out a common understanding of the nature and unity of the Church and a portrait of the kind of visibly united Church with diversity to which Anglicans and Lutherans are committed. The portrait of unity is very close indeed to that of *The Meissen Common Statement* and rests upon the same multilateral statements of the World Council of Churches. Next comes a series of twelve agreements in faith which again harvest the fruits of bilateral and multilateral conversations. The significant difference in Porvoo is that there was no need to record outstanding differences on *episkope* and episcopacy or on apostolicity and succession. Instead there is a substantial agreed theological statement on episcopacy in the service of the apostolicity of the Church.

The firm theological agreements led to the Anglican Churches of Britain and Ireland and the Nordic and Baltic Lutheran Churches (with the exception of Latvia and Denmark) ratifying a Declaration. Because this agreement includes the establishment of a single ministry in the historic succession, it has implications for the conciliar life of the Anglican Communion.

In signing the Declaration the Porvoo Churches acknowledge that each other's churches belong to the One, Holy, Catholic and Apostolic Church, that the Word of God is authentically preached, and that the sacraments are duly administered. There is an acknowledgement that each other's ministries are given by God and that the episcopal office is valued and maintained as a visible sign expressing the Church's unity and continuity. On the basis of these acknowledgements, a number of commitments are made: to share a common life and mission, to regard baptized members of all the churches as members of each church, to welcome ministers episcopally ordained to serve by invitation, to invite bishops to take part in the ordination of bishops, and to set up forms of collegial and conciliar consultation.

The coming into being of this new communion of Northern European Churches was celebrated in Norway, Estonia and London in 1996. A contact group was established to oversee the developing relations and prepare for regular meetings of church leaders. The Primates of the participating churches also meet every couple of years and the Archbishop of Canterbury invited each of the Lutheran Churches to send one bishop to attend the 1998 Lambeth Conference. The Porvoo Agreement has brought these churches into a communion of faith, sacraments, ministry and bonded life which is intended to strengthen the witness and mission of the Church in northern Europe.

The Fetter Lane Agreement between the Church of England and the Moravian Church in England and Ireland[8]

It is sometimes alleged that the Church of England will move to closer unity with partners across the water but not with churches of the same traditions in England. This is to misrepresent the situation. Indeed, the Meissen Agreement with the Evangelische Kirche in Deutschland does not go beyond the relationship which was already enjoyed in Local Ecumenical Partnerships in England. The Ecumenical Canons of the Church of England, which govern relationships in England, were the guidelines for what was appropriate with the Meissen churches. However, Meissen has the advantage that *The Meissen Common Statement* has both set out a theological basis for the relationship and also held out a portrait of visible unity towards which the churches are committed to move.

Moravians and Anglicans have long had an affection for each other and close relations, as records of early Lambeth Conferences illustrate. In 1986 the Moravian Church invited the Church of England to explore the possibility of moving into 'full communion'. As there is much that is unclear in the way this term is used and understood in ecumenical discussions, official conversations were set up only after this had been explored and a clearer understanding of how each church uses the term 'full communion' was reached. This led these conversations to leave behind the terminology of full communion and to distinguish between the goal of 'full visible unity' which is sought with all Christians everywhere, 'visible unity' as a relationship of communion of faith, sacraments, ministry structures and oversight to be lived between two or more churches, and significant 'steps and stages' which can be taken on the way to visible unity and full visible unity. This clarifying of the various relations helps to locate the Meissen Agreement as a significant step on the way to visible unity and the Porvoo Agreement as having reached visible unity. It shows that both relationships have further to go in seeking full visible unity with all Christians.

The report of the Church of England–Moravian Church discussions was published in 1995 as *The Fetter Lane Common Statement*.

The dynamic of the report is, once more, the same as that of *The Meissen* and *Porvoo Common Statements*. First, the portrait of full visible unity is drawn. It closely resembles that of Meissen and Porvoo, drawing upon the same inheritance of ecumenical texts and adding to them the more recently affirmed Canberra Statement – *The Church as Koinonia, Gift and Calling*. Next come agreements in faith, harvesting the results of bilateral and multilateral dialogues, this time made relevant to the very particular history and relationships of Anglicans and Moravians. Then follows a chapter which explains issues that still have to be faced: the most interesting of these is the exploration of how minority and majority churches can move to visible unity without the smaller church losing its own distinctive ethos and traditions.

It was on the basis of the agreements laid out, including a commitment to visible unity, and with a clear statement of what issues still have to be faced together, that both churches affirmed the Fetter Lane Declaration in the summer of 1996. The two-part Declaration is once more made up of a series of recognitions and commitments. To see that the commitments do not remain paper agreements, a Church of England–Moravian Contact Group has been established to progress implementation of the relationship. The Moravian Church nominates one of the ecumenical representatives on General Synod and from time to time the Moravian bishop will attend meetings of the Church of England bishops.

The Reuilly Agreement of 1999 between the French Lutheran and Reformed Churches and the British and Irish Anglican Churches

This agreement built on Meissen and shadowed its method. The text of the common statement is found in *Called to Witness and Service*,[9] which also includes a number of useful essays on the understandings of church, Eucharist and ministry in the Protestant and Anglican traditions represented in the Reuilly Agreement. Like Meissen and Fetter Lane, Reuilly involves mutual acknowledgement of the ecclesial authenticity of one another's churches, ministries and sacraments. On the basis of that mutual acknowledgement, it also commits the participating churches to work to overcome the remaining obstacles to fuller and more visible expressions of unity which would eventually result in ecclesial communion, with full interchangeability of ministries. The common statement is particularly significant for the way that it develops and refines the language of mutual acknowledgement and the distinction between this and a further stage involving interchangeability of ministries.

The Anglican–Methodist Covenant

The Covenant that was signed in the presence of the Queen on 1 November 2003 in Methodist Central Hall, Westminster, and celebrated liturgically in Westminster Abbey was the outcome of a long process of conversation and convergence between Methodists and Anglicans in England that began around the middle of the twentieth century. In March 1994 the General Purposes Committee of the Methodist Church wrote to the Council for Christian Unity of the Church of England inviting the Council to consider whether the two churches shared a goal of visible unity and, if so, to identify steps and stages on the way to that goal. In the light of these explorations it should be determined whether the time was right to move into formal conversations. The terms of the invitation were set in the context of the wider ecumenical relations in England and asked for understanding and encouragement from sister churches.

The report of these informal conversations (talks about talks), *Commitment to Mission and Unity*,[10] described a common goal of visible unity which closely resembled that in *The Meissen, Porvoo* and *Fetter Lane Common Statements*. It recognized that the visible unity that Anglicans and Methodists seek to live out together in England is simply a stage on the way to the full visible unity of the one Church of Jesus Christ.

The report enumerated ten issues which, it suggested, would need to be resolved by formal conversations. Many of these related to the ordained ministry and to Church–State relations.

Was the time right for such a formal conversation? The group was clear that the time could only be said to be right if both churches were prepared to take account of the complexities of the life of the churches today, not least the complexity entailed in the Church of England's recognition that two positions over the ordination of women may be held with integrity and the fact that its canon law does not at present provide for the consecration of women as bishops.

Before the Church of England and the Methodist Church responded in Synod or Conference to the recommendations of the report, the views of ecumenical partners were invited. The Baptist Union of Great Britain, the Moravian Church, the United Reformed Church and the Roman Catholic Church all sent in responses. In the main they welcomed the proposal that there should be formal conversations between the Church of England and the Methodist Church and expressed a willingness to be observers in the conversations. The General Synod in November 1997 voted by an overwhelming majority to enter formal conversations with a limited, attainable agenda and an open-ended time-scale. The conversations were mandated to seek to formulate a Common Statement, based on agreement in faith, which would support a Declaration of formal ecclesial acknowledgements and a series of commitments to move into a closer relationship. Ecumenical participants, including the Baptist Union of Great Britain, were invited to take an active part in the Conversations. Side by side with the formal conversations there was an informal trilateral conversation between the Methodist Church, the United Reformed Church and the Church of England. The Methodist Conference in July 1998 likewise agreed by an overwhelming majority to enter formal conversations with the Church of England.

The Baptist Union of Great Britain's Faith and Unity Executive Committee considered the request from the Church of England and the Methodist Church to provide a response to the proposals contained in *Commitment to Mission and Unity* and, accordingly, came to the mind that in principle the time was right for the Church of England and the Methodist Church to have formal conversations about unity. Within that overall principle the Baptist Union of Great Britain made the following points:

1   The Union would welcome the opportunity to provide an observer at the conversations.

2   The Union expressed a particular concern with regard to the United Reformed Church which has many Local Ecumenical Partnerships with the Methodist Church.

3   The Baptist Union rejoiced in the informal conversations between the Church of England and the Baptist Union and hoped that these might continue.

4   The special problems associated with Local Ecumenical Partnerships involving other traditions alongside the Church of England and the Methodist Church were seen as an important issue to be looked at during the conversations.

5   The Union hoped that any discussions would continue in reflection on the nature and style of the office of bishop.

6   The Baptist response noted that the relation of Church and State was a particularly important topic to be considered in the formal conversations.

The formal conversations, which took place between 1999 and 2001, produced the report *An Anglican-Methodist Covenant*.[11] Building on *Commitment to Mission and Unity*, the report identified a common understanding of the full visible unity of the Church of Christ and sought to take a significant bilateral step towards this wider goal. Within the overall framework of full visible unity, it set out areas of convergence and difference between Anglicans and Methodists in the areas of faith, sacraments, ministry and oversight. While not glossing over real differences, it discovered substantial common ground, sufficient for the formal conversations to propose a Covenant between the two churches. The Covenant is modelled on Meissen, Fetter Lane and Reuilly but is tailored to the shared history and interaction of Anglicans and Methodists in England since the ministry of John and Charles Wesley in the middle of the eighteenth century.

The Common Statement, culminating in the proposed Covenant, was commended by the Methodist Conference and the General Synod of the Church of England for study and response throughout the two churches. The response was overwhelmingly positive in the diocesan synods, running at around 95 per cent. In the Methodist Connexion, there was somewhat less enthusiasm, but still sufficient for the Covenant to come back to Conference and General Synod in July 2003 for decision. The Conference voted by 76 per cent in favour and the General Synod by 91 per cent. In endorsing the Covenant, these two bodies also mandated the setting up of a Joint Implementation Commission for a five-year period, charged with monitoring and promoting the implementation of the Covenant. The United Reformed Church is represented on the Commission. Like the agreements on which it is modelled, the Covenant creates a new relationship of mutual affirmation and mutual commitment, and looks towards further steps in visible unity, but does not itself achieve interchangeability of ministries. The Covenant is being enthusiastically taken up in many local situations, while work in the two churches on longer-term faith and order issues is being tracked at national level.

Baptist/Methodist 'Agreement on baptismal policy within Local Ecumenical Projects'

During the 1980s, with the rapid growth of Local Ecumenical Partnerships involving single congregations worshipping as one community within one church building, baptismal policy within such partnerships became a matter of concern. Many of the early constitutions of Local Ecumenical Partnerships set out the baptismal policies of the participating denominations and then left to 'pastoral practice' any issues which might arise if a person who had been baptized in infancy, but had not thereafter been actively involved within the worshipping community or proceeded to a point of commitment, sought, at a later stage, to make a response of commitment and a profession of faith through baptism as a believer. This issue was highlighted within the Yorkshire Baptist Association, which in 1983 published a discussion document *Baptismal Policies in LEPs*. This document offered three possible models, or ground rules, for baptismal practice in such situations and in the years that have followed all three models have been discussed within the wider community and tried within various Local Ecumenical Partnerships. However, the Baptist Union of Great Britain Advisory Committee on Church Relations and the Methodist Church Ecumenical Committee came to the view that a commonly accepted policy would be helpful both for the practice and discipline of the Methodist Church and for those responsible for drawing up constitutions for Local Ecumenical Partnerships. Negotiations then began which led to the adoption in 1990 of an agreement which sought to maintain the integrity of both Methodist and Baptist understandings and practices of baptism; to have a flexible and sensitive approach in this delicate area; and to maintain and develop good relationships and unity within the congregations of shared Baptist/Methodist churches. The agreement set out the existing policy and practice of both denominations and provided for a process by which candidates seeking believers' baptism who had previously been baptized in infancy and had rejected other possibilities, such as a public confession of faith and participation in a service of the renewal of baptismal vows, might be baptized. This baptism would follow consultation between the candidate, a Baptist minister, the Church Meeting, the Methodist Superintendent minister and the Church Council, and the person's name would be transferred to the Baptist roll. This agreement has been incorporated into many Baptist/Methodist Local Ecumenical Partnerships.

The Baptist Union of Great Britain/United Reformed Church Agreed Guidelines for Baptismal Policy in Local Ecumenical Partnerships

In 1994 the Ecumenical Committee of the United Reformed Church and the Faith and Unity Executive Committee of the Baptist Union of Great Britain agreed to hold conversations to see whether an agreement could be reached between the Baptist Union of Great Britain and the United Reformed Church on a baptismal policy for Local Ecumenical Partnerships. Conversations took place over a two-year period. It should be noted that the issues raised were more complex than in the discussions with the Methodist Church, not least because the United Reformed Church within its Basis of Union upholds the integrity of both baptism of infants and the baptism of those who are able to profess their own faith.

The agreement which was eventually concluded offered two ways forward. First, provision was made for those who had been baptized in infancy and sought baptism later as a believer to be baptized and placed on the Baptist roll of the Local Ecumenical Partnership. The second way forward encouraged some LEPs to seek a pastoral policy which does not distinguish members of different denominations within the local congregation. Whilst separate rolls still need to be maintained, the possibility was offered for a Local Ecumenical Partnership to follow a common policy for all members of the congregation. This approach would involve recognizing the need to refrain from appealing to either the Baptist Union of Great Britain Declaration of Principle or the United Reformed Church Basis of Union as the ultimate sanction, whether for or against a particular approach. In such cases infant baptism would be available to children whose parents or guardians were able to make a confession of faith and bring the children up in the faith and were members or regular worshippers and part of the church fellowship. Believers' baptism would be available to those who were able to confess their faith and commit their lives to Jesus Christ as Lord and Saviour. Before either infant or believers' baptism a course of preparation for parent(s) or candidate would precede the baptism. Believers' baptism would be administered to those baptized as infants only in exceptional cases when such an individual maintained a conviction about wishing to be baptized as a believer. In these cases, the individual's request could only be granted, and his or her name be placed on the Baptist membership roll, if the ministers and Church meetings of both traditions involved agreed to do so.

The Covenant Partnership Agreement between the Baptist Union of Great Britain and the Independent Methodist Connexion

The Covenant Partnership Agreement between the Baptist Union of Great Britain and the Independent Methodist Connexion, agreed in 2004, commits the two denominations to share resources and to work towards full integration of the two groups by 31 December 2009. It allows for all Independent Methodist Churches to become 'provisional Union Churches' i.e. members of both the Baptist Union of Great Britain and the Independent Methodist Connexion.

Theologically, the Partnership Agreement allows time for remaining ecclesiological issues between the two denominations to be resolved. The two denominations have already agreed that there are no fundamental differences between their outlooks on congregational government of churches, views on ministry, and attitudes to moral and ethical issues.

The main issue still to be discussed over the four years of the Covenant Partnership is the issue of baptism. Whilst some of the Independent Methodist churches baptize only believers, others practise the baptism of infants. This is the main reason why the four-year discussion phase has been built into the Agreement. Some Independent Methodist churches would be willing to merge with the Baptist Union of Great Britain immediately, but rather than split the Connexion, it is hoped that the four-year period will mean that most, if not all, Independent Methodist churches will be able to accept the Baptist Union of Great Britain Declaration of Principle and merge with the Baptist Union of Great Britain in 2009.

Baptist Union of Great Britain Declaration of Principle

The basis of this Union is:

1	That our Lord and Saviour Jesus Christ, God manifest in the flesh, is the sole and absolute authority in all matters pertaining to faith and practice, as revealed in the Holy Scriptures, and that each Church has liberty, under the guidance of the Holy Spirit, to interpret and administer His Laws.

2	That Christian Baptism is the immersion in water into the Name of the Father, the Son, and the Holy Ghost, of those who have professed repentance towards God and faith in our Lord Jesus Christ who 'died for our sins according to the Scriptures; was buried, and rose again the third day'.

3	That it is the duty of every disciple to bear personal witness to the Gospel of Jesus Christ, and to take part in the evangelisation of the world.

membership

Baptist Union of Great Britain

Mrs Faith Bowers

The Revd Myra Blyth (Co-Convener)
The Revd Dr Chris Ellis (until 2002)
The Revd Professor Paul Fiddes
The Revd Dr Steve Holmes (from 2002)

The Revd Paul Goodliff (from 2002)
Mrs Hilary Treavis (née Bradshaw)
The Revd Dr Richard Kidd (until 2002)
The Revd Dr Nigel Wright (until 2001)

Church of England

The Revd Prebendary Dr Paul Avis
(Co-Convener from 2002)
The Revd Dr Timothy Bradshaw
Dr Carole Cull
Dr Martin Davie
The Rt Revd Michael Doe
(Co-Convener until 2002)
The Revd William Gulliford
(until 2001)

notes

chapter 2 Anglican–Baptist relations: encouragement from the past

1 This is, for example, clear in the detailed records of the Broadmead Church in Bristol, an 'open' church because the Baptists refused to break fellowship with Independents, published as *The Records of a Church of Christ in Bristol 1640–1687*, ed. Roger Hayden, Bristol Record Society, 1974.

2 From Mieneke Cox, *The Story of Abingdon: An 18th Century Country Town*, M. Cox, 1999, pp. 48–9.

3 Information supplied by Peter Shepherd, 29 October 2002.

4 Supplied by Thornton Elwyn, historian of the Northamptonshire Association.

5 Notes of Church Meeting, 18 October 1789, now in Angus Library, Regent's Park College, Oxford, and cited in Raymond Brown, *The English Baptists of the Eighteenth Century*, Baptist Historical Society, 1986, p. 140.

6 Olney information supplied by David Dewey, mainly from Michael A. G. Haykin, *One Heart and One Soul*, Evangelical Press, 1994.

7 Quoted in Ken Manley, 'From William Carey in India to Rowland Hassall in Australia', *Baptist Quarterly*, April 2004, vol. 40, pp. 326ff. The manuscript letter is in the Mitchell Library, State Library of New South Wales.

8 John Leifchild, *Memoir of the late Rev. Joseph Hughes*, London, 1835, p. 219.

9 Douglas C. Sparkes, *Always Cinderella: Datchet Baptists over Two Centuries*, Datchet Baptist Church, 2001, p. 12.

10 For Brock, see Faith Bowers, *A Bold Experiment*, Bloomsbury Central Baptist Church, 1999.

11 Randall and D. Hillborn, *One Body in Christ: The History and Significance of the Evangelical Alliance*, Paternoster Press, 2001, p. 160.

12 Robert Ellis and Harry Mowvley, 'Memories of Dr West' in W. M. S. West, *Baptists Together*, Baptist Historical Society, 2000, p. 15.

chapter 4 one baptism: a Baptist contribution

1 The Faverges Statement, 1997, in Thomas F. Best and Dagmar Heller (eds), *Becoming a Christian: The Ecumenical Implications of our Common Baptism*, Faith and Order Paper 184, World Council of Churches Publications, 1999, p. 3.

2 Emil Brunner, *The Divine–Human Encounter*, SCM Press, 1944, pp. 128–35.

3 See *Believing and Being Baptized. Baptism, so-called re-baptism, and children in the church. A discussion document by the Doctrine and Worship Committee of the Baptist Union of Great Britain*, Baptist Union, 1996, p. 10.

4 Art. XL, in William L. Lumpkin, *Baptist Confessions of Faith*, Judson Press, 1959, p. 167.

5 So G. R. Beasley-Murray, *Baptism in the New Testament*, Macmillan, 1963, p. 200.

6 *Baptism in the New Testament, p. 200.*

7 *Baptism in the New Testament*, p. 204.

8 *Believing and Being Baptized*, p. 36.

9 See, for example, Alan Richardson, *An Introduction to the Theology of the New Testament*, SCM Press, 1958, p. 363.

10 *Believing and Being Baptized*, p. 46.

11 *Believing and Being Baptized*, p. 47.

12 See e.g. John Bunyan, *Differences in Judgment about Water Baptism No Bar to Communion*, London, 1673, p. 43; Daniel Turner, *A Modest Plea for Free Communion at the Lord's Table; Particularly between the Baptists and Paedobaptists*, J. Johnson, 1772, p. 6.

13 Christopher J. Ellis, *Baptist Worship Today. A report of two worship surveys undertaken by the Doctrine and Worship Committee of the Baptist Union of Great Britain*, Baptist Union, 1999, p. 23.

14 This is essentially the approach taken by *Baptism and Church Membership, with particular reference to Local Ecumenical Partnerships. A Report of a Working Party to Churches Together in England*, Churches Together in England, 1997, p. 13.

15 James D. G. Dunn, 'Baptism and the Unity of the Church in the New Testament', in Michael Root and Risto Saarinen (eds), *Baptism and the Unity of the Church*, Eerdmans Publishing/World Council of Churches Publications, 1998, pp. 82–3.

16 *Baptism, Eucharist and Ministry*. Faith and Order Paper 111, World Council of Churches, 1982. 'Baptism', paragraph 15, p. 6, under the heading 'Towards mutual recognition of baptism'. Our italics.

17 *Baptism, Eucharist and Ministry 1982-1990. Report on the Process and Responses*, Faith and Order Paper 149, World Council of Churches Publications, 1990, p. 109.

18 Max Thurian (ed.), *Churches Respond to BEM: Official Responses to the 'Baptism, Eucharist and Ministry' Text*, 6 volumes; World Council of Churches Publications, 1986–8, 1, p. 71.

19 E.g. *Believing and Being Baptized*, pp. 28-33; Paul S. Fiddes, *Believers' Baptism: an Act of Inclusion or Exclusion?* Hertfordshire Baptist Association, 1999, pp. 14–15; S. Mark Heim, 'Baptismal Recognition and the Baptist Churches', in Root and Saarinen (eds), *Baptism and the Unity of the Church*, pp. 156–9, 162–3; George R. Beasley-Murray, 'The Problem of Infant Baptism: An Exercise in Possibilities', in *Festchrift Günter Wagner*, ed. Faculty of the Baptist Theological Seminary, Rüschlikon; Peter Lang, 1994, pp. 12–13.

20 See, for example, *Baptism and Confirmation. A report submitted by the Church of England Liturgical Commission to the Archbishops of Canterbury and York in November 1958*, SPCK, 1959, pp. xii–xiii.

21 David R. Holeton (ed.), *Christian Initiation in the Anglican Communion. The Toronto Statement 'Walk in Newness of Life'. The Findings of the Fourth International Anglican Liturgical Consultation, Toronto 1991*, Grove Worship Series 118, Grove Books, 1991, 'Principles of Christian Initiation' c, p. 5.

22 *Walk in Newness of Life*, section 3.19–20, pp. 17–18. The later Anglican report *On The Way. Towards an Integrated Approach to Christian Initiation*, Church House Publishing, 1995, makes an attempt to find a way between 'sacramental completeness' of baptism and 'initiatory process'. Deliberately building on the Toronto Statement, this works out the principles stated there into practical arrangements for 'the welcome and nurture of new Christians' in the Christian community. In the case of those baptized in infancy, it regards their journey into active faith as a 'process of initiation'; but in order not to undermine the sacramental completeness of baptism, this journey is called '*Christian* initiation' rather than the 'sacramental initiation' which begins the journey: see pp. 37–8, 93.

23 *Walk in Newness of Life*, section 3.6, p. 15.

24 The next three sections follow closely the argument of Paul S. Fiddes, 'Baptism and the Process of Christian Initiation' in Stanley E. Porter and Anthony R. Cross (eds), *Dimensions of Baptism: Biblical and Theological Studies*, Sheffield Academic Press, 2002, pp. 295–303, used by kind permission of the publishers.

25 So John H. Westerhoff in John H. Westerhoff and Gwen N. Kennedy, *Learning Through Liturgy*, Seabury Press, 1978, pp. 163–9.

26 *Christian Initiation. Birth and Growth in the Christian Society*, Church of England Board of Education, 1971, pp. 27–31.

27 Karl Barth, *Church Dogmatics,* trans. and ed. G. W. Bromiley and T. F. Torrance, T. & T. Clark, 1936–77, IV/4, p. 42.

28 An early Baptist reference to following the example of Jesus in this rite is Thomas Grantham, *Christianismus Primitivus,* London, 1678, 2.2.1, p. 6.

29 Pauline texts are 2 Corinthians 1.22; Ephesians 1.13; 4.30; cf. 1 Corinthians 6.11; 12.13.

30 Dunn, 'Baptism and the Unity of the Church in the New Testament', pp. 85, 97–8; cf. James D. G. Dunn, *Baptism in the Holy Spirit*, SCM Press, 1970, pp. 131–4.

31 See 'The Apostolic Tradition of Hippolytus', XXII (reconstructed by Gregory Dix), in Max Thurian and Geoffrey Wainwright (eds), *Baptism and Eucharist. Ecumenical Convergence in Celebration*, World Council of Churches/Eerdmans, 1983, p. 8; cf. 'The Service of Holy Baptism in the Greek Orthodox Church', ibid., p. 15.

32 Alexander Schmemann, *Of Water and the Spirit*, SPCK, 1976, pp. 78–9, 103–4.

33 Aquinas, *Summa Theologiae*, 1a.43.5–7.

34 *Church Dogmatics*, pp. 39–40.

35 Dunn, *Jesus and the Spirit*, SCM Press, 1975, p. 254.

36 E.g. (i) Romans 7.4; Philippians 3.21; John 2.21; (ii) 1 Corinthians 6.15; 12.4-31; Romans 12.3-8; Ephesians 4.1-16; Colossians 1.18; (iii) 1 Corinthians 10.17, 24, 27, 29.

37 J. A. T. Robinson, *The Body. A Study in Pauline Theology*, SCM Press, 1953, pp. 51, 79; L. S. Thornton, *The Common Life in the Body of Christ*, Dacre Press, 1944, p. 298.

38 T. F. Best, *One Body in Christ*, SPCK, 1955, pp. 111–14.

39 Colossians 1.18. Behind the redaction of this song, the notion of the whole universe as the body of Christ is still visible; see Ralph P. Martin, *Colossians and Philemon*, New Century Bible, Oliphants, 1974, pp. 59, 63–5.

40 Gordon D. Fee, *The First Epistle to the Corinthians*, New International Commentary on the New Testament, Eerdmans, 1987, p. 603.

41 'The Problem of Infant Baptism', p. 5.

42 'The Problem of Infant Baptism', p. 9.

43 'The Problem of Infant Baptism', pp. 13–14. Our italics.

44 *An Anglican-Methodist Covenant. Common Statement of the Formal Conversations between the Methodist Church of Great Britain and the Church of England*, Methodist Publishing House and Church House Publishing, 2001, paras 122, 126, pp. 40–41. The report also refers to 'Baptism . . . in the context of full Christian initiation' (143, p. 45).

chapter 5 one baptism: an Anglican contribution

1 A. Lincoln, *Ephesians*, Word Biblical Commentary, Word Books, 1990, p. 241; cf. pp. 225–40.

2 John Calvin, *The Epistles of Paul to the Galatians, Ephesians, Philippians and Colossians*, trans. T. H. L. Parker, St Andrew Press, 1965, p. 173.

3 Richard Hooker, *Works*, ed. J. Keble, Oxford University Press, 1845, 1, pp. 339f. (*Of the Laws of Ecclesiastical Polity* III, i, 3–4).

4 Hooker, *Works*, 2, pp. 283f. (V, lxii, 4–5).

5 *On the Way: Towards an Integrated Approach to Christian Initiation*, Church House Publishing, 1995, p. 27 (2:25).

6 Hooker, *Works*, 2, pp. 250ff. (V, lvi, 7,9).

7 Hooker, *Works*, 2, pp. 258f. (V, lvii, 5,6).

8 Hooker, *Works*, 2, p. 257 (V, lvii, 4).

9 Stephen Sykes, *Unashamed Anglicanism*, Darton, Longman & Todd, 1995, pp. 13ff.

10 F. D. Maurice, *The Kingdom of Christ*, ed. A. Vidler, SCM Press, 1958, 2, pp. 258–88. Further on Maurice's ecclesiology see Paul Avis, *Anglicanism and the Christian Church: Theological Resources in Historical Perspective*, revised and expanded edition, T. & T. Clark, 2002, pp. 289–300.

11 Cf. W. F. Flemington, *The New Testament Doctrine of Baptism*, SPCK, 1948, pp. 25f.; G. W. H. Lampe, *The Seal of the Spirit*, Longmans, Green & Co, 1951, p. 37.

12 Beasley-Murray, *Baptism in the New Testament*, p. 60.

13 Joachim Jeremias, *The Theology of the New Testament*, SCM Press, 1971, 1, p. 56.

14 See further Paul Avis, *Christians in Communion*, Mowbray-Chapman, 1990, pp. 24–30.

15 T. F. Torrance, *Conflict and Agreement in the Church*, Lutterworth, 1959, 2, p. 113. J. A. T. Robinson, 'The One Baptism as a Category of New Testament Soteriology', *Scottish Journal of Theology* 6 (1953), p. 259; also in Robinson, *Twelve New Testament Studies*, SCM Press, 1962.

16 O. Cullmann, *Baptism in the New Testament*, SCM Press, 1950, p. 23.

17 Richardson, *An Introduction to the Theology of the New Testament*, p. 338.

18 Robinson, 'The One Baptism', p. 257.

19 Robinson, 'The One Baptism', p. 257.

20 *Believing and Being Baptized*, p. 37.

21 *Baptism and Church Membership*, p. 15.

22 Richardson, *An Introduction to the Theology of the New Testament*, p. 348.

23 *Lumen Gentium* 8, 15; *Unitatis Redintegratio* 22: W. M. Abbott (ed.), *The Documents of Vatican II*, Geoffrey Chapman, 1966, pp. 23, 33f.; 363f.

24 *Believing and Being Baptized*, p. 21.

chapter 6 oversight and continuity

1 E. B. Underhill, *Records of the Churches of Christ gathered at Fenstanton, Warboys and Hexham 1644-1720*, Hanserd Knollys Society, 1854.

2 *Relating and Resourcing. The Report of the Task Group on Associating*, Baptist Union of Great Britain, 1998.

3 *Canons of the Church of England*, 6th edition, Church House Publishing, 2000.

4 Hooker, *Of the Laws of Ecclesiastical Polity*, Book V.

5 John Smyth, *Principles and Inferences concerning the Visible Church* (1607); printed in W. T. Whitley (ed.), *The Works of John Smyth*, 2 volumes, Cambridge University Press, 1915, I, pp. 252–4.

6 The 'London' Baptist Confession, 1644, chapter xlvii, in Lumpkin (ed.), *Baptist Confessions*, p. 169.

7 Ordinal in *The Alternative Service Book 1980*, Church House Publishing, 1980.

8 *Bishops in Communion*, Church House Publishing, 2000.

9 Baptist Union of Great Britain discussion document, *Forms of Ministry among Baptists*, Baptist Publications, 1994, pp. 124–7.

10 *The Nature of the Assembly and the Council of the Baptist Union of Great Britain*, Baptist Publications, 1993, pp. 30–34.
11 *Baptism, Eucharist and Ministry,* 'Ministry', para. 26c.
12 *Together in Mission and Ministry: The Porvoo Common Statement with Essays on Church and Ministry in Northern Europe*, Church House Publishing, 1993.
13 *Forms of Ministry among Baptists*, p. 29.
14 *The Porvoo Common Statement*, p. 27.

chapter 7 apostolicity and recognition: an Anglican contribution

1 *The Canons of the Church of England*, 6th edition, Church House Publishing, 2000, p. 3.
2 Richardson, *An Introduction to the Theology of the New Testament*, p. 291.
3 F. F. Bruce, *The Epistle to the Hebrews*, Marshall, Morgan and Scott, 1964, p. 55.
4 *Apostolicity and Succession*, Church House Publishing, 1994, p. 9.
5 Specifically Article VII of the *Augsburg Confession*.
6 For details see G. K. A. Bell, *Christian Unity: The Anglican Position*, Hodder & Stoughton, 1948, ch. 2.
7 K. Giles, *What on Earth is the Church?* SPCK, 1995, p. 242.
8 Both of these texts were endorsed by the Elizabethan church and state as authorized statements of the teaching of the English church.
9 For details of such groups see C. J. Clement, *Religious Radicalism in England 1535–1565*, Paternoster Press/ Rutherford House, 1997.
10 G. E. Corrie (ed.), *Nowell's Catechism,* Parker Society/Cambridge University Press, 1853, p. 210. This catechism was published in Latin in 1570, having been authorized by Convocation in 1563.
11 *Nowell's Catechism*, p. 217.
12 The classic statement of the reasons for this belief is to be found in J. B. Lightfoot, *St Paul's Epistle to the Philippians*, Macmillan, 1891, pp. 186–234.
13 S. C. Neill, *Anglicanism*, 4th edition, Mowbray, 1977, p. 104. Italics original.
14 Hooker, *Of The Laws of Ecclesiastical Polity*, Book III.xi.16.
15 We can see this latter point, for example, in the revisions to the ordinal of *The Book of Common Prayer* in 1662, which made clearer than the original 1550 version that the order of bishops was distinct from the order of presbyters, and insisted unequivocally that all those who ministered in the Church of England had to have episcopal ordination. Previously some exceptions had been allowed to this general rule in the case of those who had received foreign presbyteral ordination.
16 M. Tanner, 'The Anglican Position on Apostolic Continuity and Apostolic Succession in the Porvoo Common Statement', in *Visible Unity and the Ministry of Oversight*, Church House Publishing, 1997, p. 110.

17 *Tract I: Thoughts on the Ministerial Commission, Respectfully Addressed to the Clergy*, quoted in Neill, *Anglicanism*, p. 258. Capitals in the original.

18 For a clear example of this latter position see C. Gore, *The Church and the Ministry*, rev. ed., Longmans, Green & Co, 1919.

19 The Church of the Augsburg Confession of Alsace Lorraine, the Evangelical Lutheran Church of France, the Reformed Church of Alsace Lorraine, and the Reformed Church of France.

20 *Called to Witness and Service: Conversations between the British and Irish Anglican Churches and the French Lutheran and Reformed Churches. The Reuilly Common Statement with Essays on Church, Eucharist and Ministry*, Church House Publishing, 1999, p. 36.

21 *Called to Witness and Service*, p. 36.

22 'We accept the authority of the canonical Scriptures of the Old and New Testaments. We read the Scriptures liturgically in the course of the Church's year. We believe that through the gospel, God offers eternal life to all humanity, and that the scriptures contain everything necessary to salvation.' *Called to Witness and Service*, p. 25.

23 'We share a common hope in the final consummation of the kingdom of God, and believe that in this eschatological perspective we are called to engage now in mission and to work for the furtherance of justice and peace. The obligations of the kingdom are to govern our life in the Church and our concern for the world. In this way the Church witnesses to the new humanity that has its origin and fulfilment in Christ.' *Called to Witness and Service*, p. 29.

24 *Called to Witness and Service*, p. 31 (this statement reflects *Baptism, Eucharist and Ministry*, p. 29).

25 *Called to Witness and Service*, pp. 31–2.

26 *Baptism, Eucharist and Ministry*, p. 29.

27 *Called to Witness and Service*, p. 21.

28 *Called to Witness and Service*, p. 22.

29 *Called to Witness and Service*, p. 23.

30 *Called to Witness and Service*, p. 23.

31 Except in the case of the Anglican–Methodist Covenant, when the language of 'affirmation' was used instead.

32 See *Called to Witness and Service*, pp. 51–7.

33 Church of England (Ecumenical Relations) Measure, 1988 (No.3), 5.2 (a).

appendix 1 ecumenical context of the conversations

1 *Called to be One*, Churches Together in England, 1996.

2 *Reports of Conversations between the Baptist World Alliance and the following: World Alliance of Reformed Churches – 1973, Lutheran World Federation – 1990, Vatican Secretariat for Promoting Christian Unity – 1988, Mennonite World Conference – 1992*, Baptist World Alliance, n.d.

3 *Baptists and Lutherans in Conversation. A Message to our Churches. Report of the Joint Commission of the Baptist World Alliance and the Lutheran World Federation*, Baptist World Alliance/Lutheran World Federation, 1990, pp. 40, 36.

4 *Conversations Around the World. The Report of the International Conversations between The Anglican Communion and The Baptist World Alliance, 2000–2005*, Anglican Communion Office/Baptist World Alliance, 2005.

5 *On the Way to Visible Unity: The Meissen Agreement,* Church House Publishing, 1992.

6 *Visible Unity and the Ministry of Oversight: The Second Theological Conference held under the Meissen Agreement*, Church House Publishing, 1997; I. U. Dalfert and P. Oppenheim (eds), *Witnessing to Unity: Ten Years After the Meissen Declaration*, Verlag Otto Lembeck, 2003.

7 *Together in Mission and Ministry: The Porvoo Common Statement with Essays on Church and Ministry in Northern Europe*, Church House Publishing, 1993.

8 *Anglican–Moravian Conversations. The Fetter Lane Common Statement with Essays in Moravian and Anglican History* (by Colin Podmore), Council for Christian Unity Occasional Paper No 5, Council for Christian Unity, 1996.

9 *Called to Witness and Service: Conversations between the British and Irish Anglican Churches and the French Lutheran and Reformed Churches. The Reuilly Common Statement with Essays on Church, Eucharist and Ministry,* Church House Publishing, 1999.

10 *Commitment to Mission and Unity. Report of the Informal Conversations between the Methodist Church and the Church of England.* GS Misc. 477, Church House Publishing/Methodist Publishing House, 1996.

11 *An Anglican–Methodist Covenant. Common Statement of the Formal Conversations between the Methodist Church of Great Britain and the Church of England*, Methodist Publishing House/Church House Publishing, 2001.

index